Migrant Dreams

T0346662

Migrant Dreams

Egyptian Workers in the Gulf States

Samuli Schielke

The American University in Cairo Press
Cairo   New York

First published in 2020 by
The American University in Cairo Press
113 Sharia Kasr el Aini, Cairo, Egypt
One Rockefeller Plaza, New York, NY 10020
www.aucpress.com

Dar el Kutub No. 10593/19
ISBN 978 977 416 956 4

Dar el Kutub Cataloging-in-Publication Data

Schielke, Samuli
Migrant Dreams: Egyptian Workers in the Gulf States / Samuli Schielke.—Cairo:
The American University in Cairo Press, 2020.
p.   cm.
ISBN 978 977 416 956 4
1.   Migrations of nations
325.09620976

1 2 3 4 5   24 23 22 21 20

Designed by Rafik Abousoliman
Printed in the United Kingdom

In loving memory of Daniela Swarowsky (1960–2019)

Bull, shake off your blinders and refuse to walk in circle
Break the gears of the water wheel . . . Curse and spit
The bull: Just one more step . . . and one more step
Until I reach the end of the trail, or the well dries up
How strange!

— Salah Jahin

CONTENTS

Acknowledgments xi

Preface xiii

1. *The Truman Show* 1

2. Traveling to Doha 5

3. Guarding the Bank 11

4. A Narrow Circle 19

5. Enduring and Resisting 29

6. Families Only 35

7. Everything Circles around Money Here 43

8. Things Money Must Buy 47

9. Dreaming of the Inevitable 53

10. To Have Other Dreams 61

11. A Bigger Prison 69

12. Until the End of Oil 77

13. Normality and Excess 83

14. Estrangement and Faith 91

15. The Shine of the Metropolis 101

Final Chapter: Economy Is Not Rational, and Fantasy Is Not Free 107

Notes 115

Bibliography 121

Index 133

ACKNOWLEDGMENTS

The ideas presented in this book are the outcome of conversations with others. I have tried to credit and acknowledge them whenever possible. My apologies to those I have forgotten. For the sake of privacy, the people about whom this book tells do not appear in it with their real names, and the names of companies and some locations have been changed.

The first version of this book was published in Arabic translation in 2017 with the title *Hatta yantahi al-naft* (Until the End of Oil) at Sefsafa Publishing House in Cairo, Egypt. As compared to the Arabic translation, which was based on an unpublished manuscript, this edition has been substantially revised and expanded by two chapters. Special thanks are due to Amr Khairy for translating, to Mohamed El-Baaly for publishing the Arabic edition, and to the readers of the Arabic edition, whose feedback has been crucial for the shaping of this English version.

My greatest thanks go to the people of the village that in this book is called Nazlat al-Rayyis, to the workers of the unnamed company in Doha whose book this is, and to my wife, Daniela Swarowsky, whose documentary film series *Messages from Paradise* provided the starting point for my research for this book, and who encouraged me to write this book in this way.

Thanks are also due to Paola Abenante, Khaled Adham, Muhammad AlAraby, Aymen Amer, Knut Graw, Kevin Eisenstadt, Alice Elliot, Paolo Gaibazzi, Omneya El-Gameel, Pascale Ghazaleh, Bettina Gräf,

Lucile Gruntz, Martin Holbraad, Amr Khairy, Aymon Kreil, Annika Lems, Aïssatou Mbodj-Pouye, Jennifer Peterson, Eman Salah, Ahmed Salem, Sertaç Sehlikoğlu, Mukhtar Saad Shehata, Nayera Abdelrahman Soliman, Manja Stephan-Emmrich, Mohamed Tabishat, Jelena Tošić, Mustafa Wafi, Dina Wahba, and Abdelrehim Youssef. Further thanks go to the participants of the study circle "Anthropological Readings on Our Contemporary World" at Bibliotheca Alexandrina in Alexandria, 2014–17, as well as to Michael Baers and Kevin Dean for copyediting, the AUC Press editors Nadia Naquib, Anne Routon, and Nadine El-Hadi for their enthusiasm and engagement toward publishing this book, and Bassem Muhammed Abu Gweili and Samia Jaheen for generously allowing me to reproduce their copyrighted materials in this book.

I have presented parts of this book at various stages of completeness to various audiences, from whose feedback and critique I have greatly profited, as follows: Leibniz-Zentrum Moderner Orient in 2009 and 2017, the European Conference of African Studies in Uppsala in 2011, SIEF conference in Lisbon in 2011, Humboldt University of Berlin in 2012, Boston University in 2016, University of Copenhagen in 2016, EASA conference in Milan in 2016, University of Bern in 2016, Nahda Art School in Cairo in 2016, El-Balad Bookstore in Cairo in 2017, Wekalet Behna in Alexandria in 2017, University of Bayreuth in 2017, the conference of the German Anthropological Association in Berlin in 2017, and the workshop "Post-2011 Arab Diasporas and Home-Making in Berlin" in 2019.

Research and writing for this book were made possible by my employments at Leibniz-Zentrum Moderner Orient and Berlin Graduate School Muslim Cultures and Societies, funded by the German Federal Ministry of Education and Research. The final stage of writing and revision was also supported by an ERC Consolidator Grant (ERC-2013-CoG, 617970, CARP) on the anthropology of revolutions and by project funding by the Fritz Thyssen Foundation on the search for a normal life.

PREFACE

What does being a migrant worker in the Arab Gulf states do to one's hopeful dreams? What kind of dreams of a good or better life motivate labor migration, and what kind of dreams do migrants learn to pursue through the experience of migration? What do those dreams—be they realistic and productive, or fantastic and unlikely—do to the social worlds of the people who pursue them?

Much like its English equivalent, the Arabic term *hilm* refers to both nighttime dreams and hopeful imaginations. While nighttime dreams are unbound by the laws and logic of the waking world, hopeful dreams imply the possibility, the desire, and the need to make them come true— such as in Martin Luther King's famous "I Have a Dream" speech. The "dream" in this second sense is a vernacular theory of aspiration. It is about having something to strive for, something to pursue. Such hopeful dreams are the stuff from which labor migration is made.

This book follows Egyptian men who migrated as workers to the Gulf, returned, then migrated again. Its focus is on conversations I have had with one man in particular, Tawfiq,[1] about his dreams and experiences over the years, combined with encounters with other people in similar circumstances, and my observations of their lives and struggles in Egypt and work sites abroad. Tawfiq and the other migrants whose knowledge and experience inform my argument have expressed to me their often sharp and critical understanding of their own condition, the dreams they pursue, and the structural constraints and potentials within which they live. With their help, I try to tell the story of a society where migratory movement to metropolitan centers dominates both the socially conservative dream of realizing a stable life lived in material comfort and other dreams that exceed the taken-for-granted social imagination of a good life.

We often think of imagination as a site of freedom, but this book's key argument is that just as the economy is not rational, the imagination is also not free. Some aspirational dreams are so compelling that it is almost impossible not to pursue them, such as marriage and house-building in Egypt. Contemporary labor migration thrives on and propels two different powers of the hopeful imagination: one that reproduces taken-for-granted values and expectations and another that may exceed them. Understood from the point of view of such aspirational dreams—some of them strange and unlikely, others very ordinary and so compelling that pursuing them becomes practically inevitable—migration emerges as a productive yet open-ended societal dynamic. On the one hand, it guides and limits the scope of migrants' imagination when wildly unrealistic dreams of quick wealth and a world of freedom and opportunities that originally may have motivated migratory trajectories become directed toward the more realistic goal of saving money for legitimate moral ends. On the other hand, the logic of social reproduction inherent in viable dreaming becomes in itself unsettled when migrant money transforms rural societies, and some migrants develop a horizon of experiences and expectations that exceeds the social imaginary of an ordinary, good life.

My inquiry is shaped by two productive tensions: the permanent condition of cyclical impermanence, with workers moving to and from the Gulf, and, second, the way migration opens up possibilities of social mobility while also creating its own pressures and conflicts. Rather than looking at either the Gulf states or Egypt, I try to think about the interrelation of the two in a world where villages across the Global South are in the process of being transformed into suburbs of the Gulf. Similarly, in analytical terms I am attempting to combine apparent opposites, developing a non-dichotomous approach where money and morals, imagination and materiality are not polar opposites or parallel worlds but exist on the same plane of reality. Working in the Gulf for money is a moral, spiritual condition, and imagination is a scarce resource.

Contrary to conventions of anthropological and other academic writing, the book does not begin with a detailed theoretical engagement with relevant literature. In the final chapter of the book, I elaborate how the proposal I make builds on existing research on migrations in the Gulf and elsewhere, different approaches to imagination, and both existential and political–economic approaches to migration. I have chosen to begin directly with the ethnographic encounter, following the leads it offers step by step. This is also in line with my conviction—and the explicit request by some of my interlocutors—that the most important task of this book is to describe how and under what conditions migrant workers live. Worldwide, migrants form the growing, often barely visible labor force that keeps wealthy societies running. In my opinion, conveying that reality in concrete terms, how it feels and what power relations enable it, is a key task to an anthropology of migration.

The outcome is a book of fifteen short chapters (followed by a theoretical final chapter), vaguely following the temporal line of both Tawfiq's trajectory and my learning process. The first chapter sets the stage with the unsettled sense of reality and simulation offered by places like Doha, Qatar, followed by a chapter that relates the prehistory of Tawfiq's migration and the different senses of movement involved in the complex Arabic vocabulary for migration. The next four chapters tell about the life of workers in a security company in Doha, the narrow circle of experience and expectation their living conditions reproduced, and the means of discontent and adaptation they drew on, in addition to the highly gendered ways in which migrants positioned themselves and were policed. Chapters 7 and 8 link the migrant condition with the power of money and the dream of marriage toward which the migrants I met were striving. At this stage, and in conversation with the workers in Doha and with some of those I spoke to after their return to Egypt, it becomes possible in Chapters 9 to 11 to think about the specific kind of dreams migration nurtures, as well as the different powers of imagination and the senses of limitation and possibility that come into play. The narrative then picks up with Tawfiq's return to Egypt, his marriage, and his search to sustain his family amid the uncertainty that followed the defeat of the 2011 revolution in Egypt. Following the emerging circular movement of many migratory trajectories, Chapter 12 begins to think more systematically about the long-term effect of migration on Egyptian society, especially in rural areas. Continuing on that course, Chapters 13 and 14 build partly on readers' feedback to the first version of this book that was published in Arabic translation in spring 2017. These discussions compelled me to think more systematically about paths of upward social mobility enabled by labor migration, along with the shifting forms of religiosity that accompany it. Finally, in Chapter 15 I conclude the narrative by reflecting on how Egyptian migrations are related to a worldwide movement that marks our time: of people from provinces to metropolises.

1

THE TRUMAN SHOW

During a short research fieldwork in 2009 with mainly Egyptian migrant workers employed at a security company in Doha, I had the following dream:

> I was in the village of Nazlat al-Rayyis in northern Egypt, taking a walk in the fields with my old friend M. Suddenly we arrived at a huge, new, high-tech office complex. The buildings, seven to ten stories high and built of dark glass and steel, formed a block in the middle of the Egyptian countryside, and at the center stood the station of an elevated high-speed train line, also brand new, which could take one to Cairo in thirty minutes instead of three hours. I said: "This is great, now I can come from Cairo to here on the high-speed line and walk to the village." M. told me that this was "the Smart Village No. 2," built as a copy of the original Smart Village on the outskirts of Cairo.[2]

Arriving at a place like Doha unsettles one's sense of reality. The way this nighttime dream brought together a spectacle of ostentatious hypermodernity and the rural setting from where two of my friends and interlocutors in Doha hail probably reflected my own confusion about the reality encountered by the migrant workers with whom I was staying.

The previous evening, I had gone with Tawfiq, who worked as a security guard at a bank in downtown Doha, to visit our mutual friend Amr, who, like Tawfiq, comes from Nazlat al-Rayyis. Amr was posted as a security guard at the Eurasian Sports Association (not its real name), where he manned the reception desk at the entrance. His work site was near the National Stadium and the Aspire Sports Academy, which are among the most conspicuously hypermodern spaces of Doha. Nearby stands Villaggio, one of the city's fanciest shopping malls. Villaggio is a simulation of Venice, its shops constructed as Disneyfied imitations of Italian houses. There is an ice-skating rink and a canal where one can take a gondola ride, and the ceiling is painted to look like the sky—blue, with white clouds and diffuse light. It was Thursday evening (the beginning of the weekend in Qatar) and the mall was full. Tawfiq and I entered to buy some food to share with Amr at his workplace.

At first, Tawfiq was intrigued, pleased to see the many attractively dressed young women strolling around, but he quickly became disturbed and, finally, appalled. He said:

> Now I realize what a good, decent place Egypt is (*addi eh Masr bint nas*, literally: how much Egypt is the daughter of good people). This is the purest falsification. This is *The Truman Show*. I have never missed Egypt as badly as I do now.

Two things upset Tawfiq. For one thing, Villaggio is an extreme display of conspicuous consumption, an insult flung in the face of the conditions of exploitation Tawfiq and his fellow migrant workers faced in Qatar. Tawfiq had to count every penny of his meager salary. Like other migrant workers I met, he was extremely price conscious, becoming angry at the thought of anyone, rich and poor alike, spending more money than was necessary. Conspicuous consumption was an offense against both his position in the system and his main goal in being there: saving money for his future.

Second, Tawfiq hated the mall because it was such a comprehensive simulation. Comparing the mall with the Hollywood film *The Truman Show* (1998), in which the hero Truman is the unknowing star of a reality television show, Tawfiq described it as a fake, artificial world that made it impossible to find any footing in the real world (which he explicitly located in Egypt). His observation echoes a concept that has gained currency in the study of the Arab Gulf: hyperreality.

Hyperreality (Baudrillard 1993; Steiner 2014; Wippel et al. 2014) is a form of simulation so convincing that the original appears less real. Regarding the ambitious construction projects in Gulf cities, the air-conditioned worlds of luxury and material pleasure, the skyscrapers rising along the coastline in past years, and the combined sense of awe and disorientation these structures often generate, there is certainly something to be said for applying the notion of hyperreality when trying to understand them. Had Tawfiq known about the concept, he well might have used it. Had he been familiar with the work of the geographer Yasser Elsheshtawy, he would also have likely agreed that prestige projects in the Gulf cities are indeed "spectacles" (in the sense of Debord 1977), where ultimately "falseness becomes a virtue, a model" (Elsheshtawy 2013, 112).

Tawfiq's anger at the sight of Villagio mall reminds us that there is another, darker side to the hyperrealities of the Arab Gulf (see also Elsheshtawy 2010). They are built, maintained, and serviced by a labor force that lives in a very different sort of reality from the glass and steel palaces along the coast. Tawfiq described the contrast through another popular cultural reference, the science fiction novel *Utopia* by Egyptian writer Ahmad Khaled Towfiq (2008; 2011). His book is a nightmare vision of extreme class polarization, where the rich live in the isolated city of "Utopia," protected by high walls separating it from the extreme misery on the outside. Tawfiq explained: "Doha is also such a utopia. As for the other side of the utopia, that is the dystopia where we live."

If the sports park and the Villagio mall were prime examples of utopian hyperreality, the daily life of Tawfiq and his colleagues might be described as a kind of *hyporeality*, a dystopian existence that is somehow less than real: a dim state of routine, focused on something other than the immediate material spot in which they are present—a life of enduring for the sake of something other than this.

However, concepts like hyperreality or "hyporeality" only take us so far. They may help us to understand the powerful effect of the Gulf as a dream world where everything seems possible. But unlike Baudrillard's hyperbolic "desert of the real," fantasies often do not take one away from reality; rather, they change reality. Falseness may be a virtue in shopping malls, yet they structure the material ways in which people actually move, eat, shop, and work. They make some people rich while providing others a meager income. The aspirations of migrant workers ordinarily involve more mundane projects: home, marriage, family. The workers' less-than-real sense of existence in Doha was intrinsically connected to an immensely productive process of realizing things at home; they were building lives somewhere else.

This is what I try to trace in the following chapters: the dialectics of the pressing dream of movement and advancement; the experience of the life of the migrant, which is felt to not really be a life yet is entirely concerned with building a life; the troubled temporality of a constantly deferred future, as produced by this dialectic under the conditions of an oppressive labor regime; the tangible material effects that migrants' strivings have; and, last but not least, the way those material effects in turn shape new dreams. This process is especially pronounced among low-income migrant laborers relocating to the Gulf states on temporary contracts, and it is this group my book discusses. The concrete questions I try to answer are as follows. What does being a migrant worker do to one's dreams? And what impact do those dreams have on the world in which one lives?

2

TRAVELING TO DOHA

International and rural–urban migration is close to a total social fact in Egypt, second only to marriage, the military state, and the worship of God. According to the 2017 national census, one out of eleven Egyptians currently resides abroad. Two-thirds of the Egyptians abroad live in other Arab countries, mainly in Saudi Arabia, Jordan, and the United Arab Emirates. Other large Egyptian diasporas can be found in the United States, Canada, and Italy (*Mada Masr*, 2017). In Tawfiq's home village, most migrants go to Saudi Arabia or other Arab Gulf states. In the neighboring town, Italy is the main destination. In Tawfiq's extended family,[3] nine of the ten men born between 1960 and 1990 have been international migrants at some stage in their lives. By summer 2019, five of them were currently living abroad. (In a remarkable gender contrast, Tawfiq's sister is the only woman in the extended family—not counting spouses—who has thus far lived or worked abroad.)

Egypt is a migrant nation, but it does not convey a sense of free-floating movement. For the vast majority of Egyptians, moving across borders is difficult, costly, and full of risks. This difficulty of movement makes it even more loaded with promises and expectations. This is in no way unique to Egypt, of course. While increasing migration across borders is met by increasing visa restrictions and border controls, the dream of migration to the North has become only more compelling throughout the Global South (see, for example, Alpes 2012; Elliot 2015; Swarowsky 2014).

However, there are different ways to be held back by borders and to cross them, and there are different experiences of living abroad. Class makes an enormous difference. Less class privilege generally means more limited possibilities of movement and more exploitative and alienating conditions of living abroad—be it as an undocumented migrant or asylum seeker in Europe or as a low-income contract worker in the Gulf. Visa and labor regimes are equally of consequence. The Gulf states offer temporary work visas on all income levels and do not criminalize low-income workers as illegal or irregular residents as systematically as European and North American states often do (Menin 2017; de Genova 2002). However, attaining legal residence is governed by highly exploitative laws, most importantly the sponsorship *(kafala)* system (more about this in the next chapter). Significantly, Gulf states usually do not allow migrant workers to stay after retirement. Low-income "migrant" laborers and top-salary "expat" functionaries alike are subject to a circular logic of temporary work contracts and ultimate return to their home countries.[4]

Some differences are also due to the specific aims and stages of one's movement. In this regard, Arabic is endowed with a migration-related lexicon that is helpful in understanding some of the specific qualities of moving to and living in a place far from home.[5]

The Arabic word for migration, *hijra*, is not identical in use with the English "migration," except in some academic and policy uses. *Hijra* usually implies leaving a place behind with the intention of settling permanently in a new place. It also has a religious connotation due to Prophet Muhammad and his followers' emigration *(hijra)* from Mecca to Medina that transformed Muslims from a small persecuted group into an expansionist world religion. Egyptians living and working in the Gulf states would not be likely to see themselves as *muhajirin* (permanent settler–emigrants), because they know that sooner or later they will return home. In legal terms, they are described in the Gulf states as residents *(muqimin)* or arrivals *(wafidin)*, in opposition to citizens *(muwatinin)*.

They and their families and friends, however, would more likely say that they are *mughtaribin* (living away from home) or *musafirin* (traveling).

A *mughtarib* is somebody who lives in *ghurba*, which means the sense of being abroad in a strange place among strangers, separated from the familial connections and safety of home. To experience *ghurba* or "strangerhood" is to live a life that is not full in the relational sense and that lacks the comfort of the familiar. It is a notion that stands in marked contrast to the much more open-ended concept of *safar*, meaning travel, departure, and migration. *Safar* is associated with the promise and possibility of movement, while *ghurba* is the condition of disconnection from a full life that one may have to endure as a consequence of that movement. *Safar* is something one may pursue, *ghurba* something one must endure. Notably, the philosophical concept of alienation in Arabic is expressed by the term *ightirab*, which also means the act of moving away from home to a state of *ghurba*. Neither *ghurba* nor *safar* carry the connotations of rupture and permanence that *hijra* possesses. One can travel (*yisafir*) for a week or for the rest of one's life. One can live in *ghurba* for decades and never feel that the place one inhabits is home.[6] A few Egyptians have also told me that they experience *ghurba* in their homeland in the sense that they feel alienated, unwell, and unrecognized in it.

Tawfiq and others in similar positions thus did not emigrate (*yihajir*) to the Gulf in the sense of aiming to make it their new home. Some of them might have dreamed (and Tawfiq indeed did) of becoming a *muhajir* (emigrant) to America or Western Europe. However, the actual path of *safar* (travel) they undertook brought them to the alienating and exploitative condition of *ghurba* (strangerhood): workers hired on temporary contracts in the Gulf states, their efforts devoted to saving money in order to build a life at home that had yet to begin. As I speak about migrants in this book, I therefore (unless otherwise specified) mean the *mughtaribin* who understand their condition as one of a temporary (while possibly long-lasting) migrancy away from home.

Tawfiq's first *safar* took him to Qatar, where he worked for two years (2008–10) as a security guard for an international company. The site and kind of work were both coincidence: his friend Amr, who is several years older and needed to save money for his marriage, had received a contract as a guard some months earlier, and Tawfiq followed him. Both Tawfiq and Amr come from relatively poor, rural families in Nazlat al-Rayyis. They have some higher education and great expectations, but their resources were only sufficient to get low-pay, public-sector jobs in Egypt. Amr is a schoolteacher, while Tawfiq is a health inspector. Incidentally, they are both literature enthusiasts and writers: Tawfiq writes poetry and Amr writes short stories.

Tawfiq had dreamed of leaving Egypt since he was young. When I first became better acquainted with him in 2006, he was already developing plans for migration, or "escape," as he often called it. He had originally wanted to go to either the United States or Western Europe, but a path to emigrate to those countries was unavailable to him (and he refused to take the risk of crossing the Mediterranean on a fishing boat). I also could not organize a visa for him. Thus, he settled for a contract in Doha in the hope that it might be a stepping stone on his imagined path to Europe or America. The dreams he invested in *safar* (travel) comprised the desire and need to fulfill the social expectation that he become a mature adult and responsible family man, along with a pressing need for money, accentuated by the relative poverty of his family. There was also a personal as well as political desire for freedom, new experiences, and knowledge. However, his actual migrations have so far all taken place in the limited and limiting framework of labor contracts in the Arab Gulf states: the first two times as a security guard and the third time as a customer service representative.

Much of Tawfiq's life trajectory and experience is common, even typical. He belongs to a vast mainstream in Egypt's population, a group that is for the most part relatively young, possessing some formal education and being poor but hopeful. People like Tawfiq are systematically excluded from the well-paid jobs and mobility that wealthy Egyptians can take for granted. After completing his two-year higher vocational education, he received a badly paid government job as a health inspector—a position that provides a meager yet stable salary but no lucrative side income, as some other public-sector jobs do. He migrated as a worker to the Gulf, returned, got engaged, migrated again, got married, became a father, and migrated once again. He has recently begun building a house with his income from abroad.

In other ways, Tawfiq is a peculiar, exceptional person. Politically, he is a socialist and an admirer of the Cuban revolution—something uncommon in rural Egypt. He married the daughter of a senior Communist activist from a nearby village. Their marriage was the outcome of a love story, which they celebrated publicly—also not an ordinary thing to do in rural Egypt. He comes from an extended family who once were fishermen and who still identify as such. They own little to no land or other material resources but value culture and education highly. Some of his cousins have made it to reasonably well-paid urban careers in media and education. He is a poet who writes modernist verse in classical Arabic. He is also an excellent observer and analyst of his own society and has always been very interested to share his knowledge with me. This has made him one of my most valued friends and interlocutors in Egypt over the years.

Tawfiq had already participated in some of my earlier ethnographic research about the month of Ramadan, boredom, and dreams of migration (Schielke 2015; Swarowsky and Schielke 2009). When he departed for Qatar, I was interested to learn what the reality of being a migrant worker meant for a young man whose greatest dream until then had been to leave Egypt and to live a life in freedom and comfort.

With just three weeks available to me in October and November 2009, my field research in Doha was brief and intense. I spent it almost entirely among workers of a security company, most of them Egyptian, some Nepalese. Often anthropologists need to spend a long time to get

access to a field site and to build a relationship with research participants, but I was lucky in having Tawfiq as my guide. My research time in
Doha began almost immediately after arriving at the airport, continuing
practically uninterrupted until the hour of my departure.[7]

In contrast to the brevity of my visit to Doha, in Egypt I have
remained in contact with Tawfiq and Amr on a regular basis for more
than ten years, both before their departures and after their returns to
Egypt. I have also spoken and visited, albeit less regularly, with other
workers whom I met in Doha. I have accompanied them as they have
built their houses, gotten married, returned from contracts, and sought
out new ones. And I have witnessed the gradual transformation of Tawfiq's home village of Nazlat al-Rayyis and the movements of some of its
other inhabitants over the course of the last two decades. Tawfiq and
Amr read and commented on the first draft of the Arabic version of this
book before it was released in January 2017. Tawfiq and his wife, Zarqaa,
also advised me regarding this revised English edition.

But Tawfiq could not come to the book launch of the Arabic edition in Alexandria in February 2017. He had just departed for his third
contract abroad. His absence in particular was a painful reminder of the
structural asymmetries that anthropology is part of, despite the best
intentions of researchers. For me, *safar* (travel) for fieldwork has always
been an intense, engaging, and fulfilling experience. Tawfiq's *safar*, in
contrast, brought him the rather troubling condition of *ghurba* (strangerhood) that has by now become a cyclical reality in his life. Could I
have helped him get a better chance? Is it enough for this book to simply
fulfill the promise that I tell about the conditions of living and working
in Qatar? Hardly, but let it be a beginning.

3

GUARDING THE BANK

Tawfiq, Amr, and their many colleagues worked for the Qatari branch of a major international security corporation. They were assigned for various durations to different work sites, such as banks, parks, public buildings, or the Doha airport. I spent most of my time with guards working in two banks in Grand Hamad Street, near the old center of Doha.

Regular guards were mostly young and unmarried; at least in the case of the Egyptian security guards, their primary aim was usually to save money in order to get married. Head guards and supervisors who had worked for the company for upward of five years usually had families back home. The company employed people from several countries, including Egypt, Nepal, Sri Lanka, India, Thailand, and Sudan.

The security company, which was owned partly by a parent company headquartered in Western Europe and partly by Qatari investors, sold its services to customers such as banks and government institutions. In 2009, the Bank of Oceania (not its real name), where Tawfiq worked, paid the security company 3,500 Qatari riyals (approximately 710 euros at the time) per month for a guard working a twelve-hour shift, seven days a week. His share was 1,100 riyals (approximately 225 euros at the time), plus accommodation and transportation—minus the fees for the labor agent and the visa, which amounted to a one-time cost of 6,000 riyals. Additionally, the bank directly paid the guards a monthly allowance of 250 riyals, which made the Bank of Oceania well liked among the guards.

The jobs in which Tawfiq and Amr were employed are part of a complex network of global trade in energy, services, labor, and finance. They got their contracts through labor agents who are active in their countries of origin. They worked for an international corporation selling its services to financial institutions, who, in turn, made a profit by formulating investment schemes to administer and reinvest the abundant oil and gas income of the Qatari state. Their work conditions were predicated upon a labor regime that is a specialty of the Arab Gulf states, one that gives employers almost unlimited power over employees. It is a system that provides good returns for investors worldwide. If, by chance, you have savings invested in the shares of multinational companies, you are a direct profiteer of this system.

The work in the Bank of Oceania consisted of manning the reception desk at the employees' entrance, guarding the entrance to the car park, sitting at a customer service desk at the customers' entrance during business hours, occupying the control room where the CCTV screens are located, and opening the door for the director of the bank when he arrived in the morning. Occupying a reception or customer service desk were among the most popular tasks, because these were the least lonely and monotonous of the work assignments available. Compared to guarding a garage entrance or manning a control room, at a reception desk there was more going on and there were many occasions for social interaction.

The work was not hard, unless one had to work outdoors in the hot Gulf climate. The guards described their relationship with the bank employees as cordial, even friendly. When the bank was closed, the guards were allowed to smoke inside the building. But the work was monotonous and boring, the shifts were twelve hours long, and the pay was bad. The men were often exhausted. Tawfiq slept badly and lost weight. Ali, who worked at a different site but lived in the same accommodation, pointed out the following:

When you work a twelve-hour shift, you have no time or energy. When I come back from work, I eat, take a shower, and pray the evening prayer and then you're already so tired that you can only sleep, and at 4:30 your phone's alarm clock wakes you up again. Working a twelve-hour shift leaves you no time or energy to care about anything.

The guards officially had one day off per week, but they all worked seven days a week because a day off was a day without pay, while working on weekends meant more money. Even easy and undemanding work wears one down when it goes on twelve hours every day, month after month, year after year. But it was more than duration that made the work grinding. Most of the guards found their work completely pointless. Consequently, they were bored and demotivated. Most importantly, they were dissatisfied with their pay and contract conditions.

Across the street from the Bank of Oceania stood the Bank of Eastasia (also not its real name), where Tawfiq knew many of the guards because contract employees often moved back and forth between the two work sites. Many friends of Tawfiq worked there: the Egyptians Sayf, Girgis, and Hamza and the Nepalese Lokraj. On one of the occasions we crossed the street to meet them for lunch or a chat, Tawfiq pointed out to me jokingly that I was now "a friend of the security [staff]." "Funny," I replied to him, "I'm spending all my time with security guards here, but security is not an issue at all." Tawfiq responded, "It's because nobody cares about security. We're here only for show. We're totally useless."

I heard of no cases where any of the sites where the guards worked would have been exposed to immediate danger or trouble. The most dramatic event I heard of involved two bank employees who got caught having sex in the lift after work hours. Qatar is a very safe place, where the most serious security work is related to policing the migrant workers; that work was done by a different company and the police.[8]

At the Bank of Eastasia, Hamza—in contrast to Tawfiq—was well motivated and worked hard. He enjoyed his work, but it also made him angry. In only a short time, he had risen to a responsible position within the bank. He was posted in the control room and told that he was actually doing a good portion of his boss's job. His boss, a Qatari, didn't work much, delegating to the guards even highly responsible work, including passwords. The bright side of his boss's indolence, Hamza told me, was that it offered him interesting responsibilities where he could learn something. He even had some authority over regular bank employees. But he also pointed out that as a guard working for the company, he was paid a fraction of what Qatari employees of the bank received in salary. Hamza said:

> This is the way with every Qatari employee: They sleep and let the migrant workers—Egyptian, Indian, Nepalese—do the work . . . for a fraction of the money that should be paid for the work. That's *haram* [forbidden, wrong]. It's more than *haram*, if I could only think of a word that would be even stronger than *haram*.

Hamza's Nepalese colleague Lokraj argued that Hamza took his work too seriously. He agreed, however, that the pay was totally inadequate. Lokraj previously worked in Nepal as a tour guide (and thus speaks good English). He had a wife and three children in Nepal. As a tour guide, he said, he could earn seasonally as much as he does here, but only during the tourist season, which is why he was in Qatar. But, he complained, the combination of bad pay, the high cost of living, and the lack of rights made it hard to save any money:

> We guards all earn the same (1,100 riyals), but life is very expensive here. The top employees of the bank earn 200,000 riyals, and they buy their food in the same supermarket as we do. And the problem is that we have no rights here. If I go to court and demand my rights, I will be thrown out of the country. And I cannot change the *kafil* [sponsor] to go to another job. There are other security companies that would pay 3,000 riyals, but we are not allowed to change.

The *kafil*, a migrant worker's sponsor, was the key figure looming over the guards' predicament. Non-citizen workers in most Gulf countries are required to have a local sponsor who is their legal guardian during their stay.[9] Without the sponsor's agreement, one cannot buy a car, get married, leave the country, or take another job. The treatment of workers under the *kafala* (sponsorship) system has been the source of much criticism by human rights organizations and the international media (Human Rights Watch 2008; 2009; 2012; Motaparthy 2014; Karlsson 2014). In reaction to public scrutiny into the situation of workers building sports facilities prior to the 2022 World Cup, and perhaps also to improve Qatar's public profile in the context of the political conflict with and blockade by Saudi Arabia and the United Arab Emirates, in 2017 Qatar began to reform its labor laws. Workers are now allowed to change their sponsor, but only after completing their previous contract (Business & Human Rights Resource Centre 2018). However, Qatar and the other Gulf countries are unlikely to fundamentally change a system from which they profit enormously. In both its full-scale and reformed variations, *kafala* keeps salaries low and sets strict limits to workers' rights.[10]

In 2009, there were other security companies in Qatar that paid significantly better wages, but the sponsor for the workers in the company I followed—a high-ranking member of the royal family with tens of thousands of workers under his guardianship—systematically refused every worker's request for a change in workplace or a transfer to another sponsor. This was very profitable for the company: it could pay low wages and still be certain that its workers—who were always recruited directly from countries like Egypt, Nepal, or Thailand and never hired on the spot in Qatar—could not resign from their contracts and wander off to better-paying companies.

In addition to being subject to the sponsor's authority, workers were and still are prohibited by contract and law from forming trade unions or organizing strikes. Workers had no realistic legal recourse for claiming unpaid salaries, which is why companies often left their employees unpaid for months. The company where my friends worked was considered punctual in payment: salaries usually arrived with one week's delay. The punishment for any attempts to resist the labor regime is simple. Offenders are "canceled"—that is, their contracts and visas are terminated, and they are swiftly expelled. For the workers, this is a heavy punishment, meaning a loss of the income they came to Qatar for in the first place. The prospect of instant cancellation and deportation overshadows the lives of all non-citizens working in Gulf states, including high-income employees.

These policies add up to a system engineered for maximum exploitation, and it works exceedingly well. Consequently, the security contractor made ample profit from its workforce, while its employees ended up saving a sufficient amount to keep working, but less than they had anticipated. There was nothing they could do about the situation other than quitting and returning home. And as one of the supervisors pointed out, security guards were not even the most exploited workers: "There are people here who work for 500 riyals—domestic workers and cleaners, for example. That is so little money, it is not enough for anything."

Not all migrant laborers suffer equally under this regime. Amr enjoyed his employment at the Eurasian Sports Association (where he was lucky enough to work an eight-hour shift instead of the usual twelve-hour one), had good relations with others at his workplace, and remembered his years in Qatar with fondness afterward. He was dissatisfied with his salary and as a result had to stay one year longer than planned, but eventually he did manage to save enough to return to Egypt and marry in 2010. Tawfiq, by contrast, was often disappointed, angry, and depressed. Like Amr, he saved some money, but at a rate so slow he didn't feel it made much difference. Both physically and mentally he was in bad shape, as were many others whom I met: strained by habitual monotony; under pressure from the meagerness of the wage, which made the whole business of working abroad seem so futile; angered by the injustice they faced; and accompanied constantly by a strong sense of homesickness and alienation caused by living a less-than-real life that provided less real income than they had imagined.

4

A NARROW CIRCLE

The guards' life mostly revolved around a narrow circle that consisted of the work site, the accommodations provided by the security contractor, occasional walks to buy food at a shopping mall, calling home, and going online. They rarely ventured outside this circle, because doing so would cost money, because they were exhausted after their twelve-hour shift, and because they had limited access to transportation.

Although cars are cheap in Qatar, none of the regular guards could afford one. Some of the supervisors had private cars and also lived in more comfortable accommodations. They earned 1,500 riyals before allowances and extras—400 more than regular guards, but still way too little to even think about sending for their families to come live with them in Doha. Without access to a private car, one's movement in Doha's motorized urban space is very limited. The guards rarely used public buses, which are slow and cost money, but they could rely on the network of company shuttles that departed from different work sites at different times. When the company minibuses were unavailable, they would walk. On my visit, we often walked long distances in the nighttime, going to the shopping mall or visiting workers housed in other accommodations. These walks and rides in the company minibus were among the most important social occasions in the narrow circle of a guard's life, but they usually went in a closed circle, from one often-visited station to another.

This circle was marked by conflicts, alienation, and the dull experience of a less-than-real existence. But it also provided an urgently needed sense of friendship and belonging. The most important site for the latter was the workers' accommodation.

In 2009, the company had several accommodations in various residential districts of the city. The company frequently opened new accommodations and closed old ones. Consequently, workers were often moved from one place to another. The accommodation where I stayed with Tawfiq was located in a recently built residential area in the south of Doha, some twenty minutes' distance from the bank via company shuttle.

The accommodations housing male guards (supervisors and female guards had separate accommodations) consisted of two buildings of three floors each, with a small open area between the houses and the outer wall. On the top floor, there was a small open courtyard. In front of the building, there was a three-meter-wide oasis of plants that thrived on the water from a leaking sewage tank that emitted a distinct odor. The whole complex had been given a fresh coat of paint within and without just days before my arrival, but the rooms still looked old and worn out, and the bathrooms and kitchens were even more dilapidated. The sleeping rooms, which varied in size and held different numbers of people and beds, had air-conditioning, and the building had hot water.

The room where Tawfiq stayed was smaller than most rooms. It had two bunk beds and one single bed (regular guards slept in bunk beds, while head guards were entitled to single beds), all of which were occupied. I slept in the bed of a guard who worked the night shift.[11] The window was covered with a piece of cardboard so that night-shift workers could sleep in the daytime. Foodstuffs were located close to the ceiling in plastic bags, on account of cockroaches. The building was infested with bedbugs, making life difficult, especially in the summer heat. Guards' uniforms hung on the walls, bags were stowed underneath the beds and in two small cupboards, and small curtains covered the lower bunk to provide a minimum of privacy. On the walls hung a few prayers and Qur'anic verses; on the ceiling were colored strips of a Ramadan decoration. There was a soft and reasonably clean carpet on which the workers would usually sit when they were eating or socializing. In other rooms, workers often used Qatari flags as curtains for the lower beds (the flags were distributed to the workers free of charge upon arrival). Almost all rooms had a television set, but Tawfiq's room was an exception. For entertainment, they relied on movies downloaded to Tawfiq's laptop. The few books I saw were all religious, save for a pile of Arabic literature and translations belonging to Tawfiq, who spent much of his free time reading.

The rooms were distributed according to nationality. On the floor where Tawfiq resided, all three rooms housed Egyptians. The top floor had rooms housing Nepalese workers and one room housing three men from Sudan. The ground floor was occupied mostly by people from Thailand; the other building mainly housed Indians and Sri Lankans. The rooms I saw were more or less similar in layout, very crowded, and mostly not particularly clean. The room of the three Sudanese guards was an exception. They had already lived in Qatar for some time and had a room to themselves, with three single beds, a clean carpet, and a low table in the middle of the room. It stood out as exceptionally clean and cozy.

One of the neighboring buildings had open wireless internet access, and everybody with a laptop tapped into it.[12] The network only worked outdoors, and so in the evening the Egyptian guards would climb to the roof of their accommodation—their cybercafé, as they jokingly called it—to maintain contact with friends, families, girlfriends, and brides, as well as to download music and films. (The photograph on the cover of this book shows one of those gatherings on the roof.) In October, the air was already comfortably cool in the evenings, and on several occasions I climbed with Tawfiq and the others up to the roof, where we sat talking and joking, listening to music, and watching TV in a pleasant atmosphere. But they wouldn't have climbed up to the roof if not for the wireless connection.

Most guards cooked their own food—among them Amr, who told me that while he disliked cooking, it saved him money and that having fresh, hot food made life much more bearable. Adham, the head guard who lived in the same room as Tawfiq, also cooked his own food. Adham told me that he observed a strict daily routine: he could not sleep unless he prayed the evening prayer and had a shower. The shower, he added, was related to his passion for sports and his education as a sports teacher, whereby he had developed the habit of taking a shower to mark the transition between exercise and rest. Others, among them Tawfiq, relied on fast food that they bought at a small shopping area nearby and had a less routinized pattern of life. At least for Tawfiq, this more irregular pattern was accompanied by bad sleep, exhaustion, and times of depression.

Crowded, dirty, and unhomely as it was, the accommodation was nevertheless the best thing in the guards' life, a space of socialization and friendship. Tawfiq stated at one point that although there were often conflicts and tensions resulting from living in such proximity to other men, being together in the accommodation made life bearable: "At least we have each other," he said.

But the workers were not unified in their function as workers. They were unified as *Egyptian* workers.

One evening, I took the company minibus with Tawfiq from the bank to the accommodation. The minibus was filled to capacity, mostly with Egyptian, Nepalese, and Indian guards. One of the Nepalese guards was late, and the driver, who was Nepalese or Indian, wanted to wait. The Egyptians got nervous and angry, telling the bus driver in Arabic, "You son of a bitch, what are you waiting for?" Minutes later, the man arrived and the minibus drove off, but the atmosphere remained tense and the Egyptians continued expressing their opinions to each other, still in Arabic, their speech accompanied by one obscene insult after another. The previous evening, I had been sitting in the same minibus and one of the Egyptians had been late.

That time, the Nepalese and Indians got nervous and the driver wanted to depart without the missing Egyptian: the Egyptians insisted he should wait.

On an individual level, workers from different nationalities could be friendly and respectful toward each other. But in situations such as a waiting minibus preparing to depart at the end of a long workday, people almost invariably acted as a bloc, standing by their countrymen, and the atmosphere could quickly become aggressive and disrespectful. There was a proliferation of racist jokes and comments about other ethnic groups. Having one another can make life bearable, but the dependence on group solidarity also implies the establishment of mutually antagonistic groups, drawn along ethnic and national lines. This is why rooms in the company accommodation were almost always segregated by nationality. Mixed rooms would be too prone for conflicts about the smell of food and standards of privacy and interaction. Religious sensibilities were a part of this segregation but only insofar as they were congruent with nationality and ethnicity. There was some solidarity among people from Arab countries, but Egyptian and Sudanese guards lodged in separate rooms, and the one Moroccan worker in the accommodation lived in a room where everybody else was from Thailand.

Food in particular was an important and morally loaded concern. The Egyptian workers would never eat South Asian food, with the exception of chicken sandwiches that were sold cheaply near the bank. In Qatar, all low-cost food is *halal*, so that was not the issue. The very sight and smell of South Asian food and eating habits struck the Egyptians as wrong, unsettling their sense of bodily and moral well-being—a sense intimately connected with food and eating. The Egyptians even took issue with the fact that I liked to frequent cheap Pakistani or Nepalese food joints for lunch. To my Egyptian friends, my taste for South Asian food raised question marks about my loyalty toward them.

For Tawfiq, migration was never only about saving money but also about expanding his horizon, learning to find his way in different parts of the world, with different people. For many migrants, the experience of dealing with people from different ethnic, religious, and class back-grounds contributes to a cosmopolitan skillfulness in dealing with people from different places (el-Aswad 2004; Stephan-Emmrich 2017). I did meet Egyptians who said that they had learned and profited from con-tact with people from India or the Philippines, with their surprising and strange habits and beliefs. But only a minority explicitly embraced the diversity of a place like Doha. More often, worldliness—knowing one's way in the metropolis—coexists with the search to live among one's own kind in purity and segregation, avoiding close contact with people whose different ways and values might be a source of disturbance or discomfort (Osella and Osella 2007). For people occupying higher income levels, class segregation often makes it easier to cross ethnic boundaries (see Kanna 2010; Vora 2013). People in the low-income sector, however, are more heavily dependent on ethnic communities for support. Tawfiq did have good relations with his Nepalese colleagues in Qatar, and one of his best friends, Lokraj, was Nepalese. And yet his relationship with the plurality of different lifestyles, languages, ethnicities, and cultural back-grounds he encountered in Doha was often marked by the same attitude that I encountered among most Egyptian guards: a degree of suspicion toward the unknown and unfamiliar in general, coupled with a preju-diced and ridiculing attitude toward other nationalities.

Prejudice works by establishing a double standard between group stereotypes and individual recognition: Tawfiq pointed out to me that Lokraj was different from the other Nepalese, while Lokraj told me that Tawfiq was unlike the other Egyptians.

Lokraj worked at the entrance to the car park behind the Bank of Eastasia, handing out parking receipts as cars entered. At noon one day I visited him there. He complained to me about how Egyptians deal with other nationalities. "They shout and laugh and command and say *khalli walli* to you," he said, using a term that I discuss in more detail in the next chapter. He added that not everybody was like this. Tawfiq, for example, did not behave this way, and of the thirteen or fourteen Egyptians he had worked with previously, only one had treated him poorly. But still, he insisted, the Egyptians were not well liked by other nationalities. A car entered the garage. The driver asked Lokraj something and he replied in Arabic, "Fourth floor." Then he said to me in English:

> I have learned some words of Arabic here, but most of the Egyptians learn nothing. Tawfiq is one of the few people who speaks a few words of Nepalese, and good English. Most of them don't even try to learn English or any other languages. We come here to a strange country in a different culture, we have to bear with it. We have to bear with a lot of things, but they don't know how to bear with different people. I don't know whether it has to do with the families, how they grow up, but they have a way of commanding people around. In Nepal, if you travel there for a day, you will meet a lot of people, they are friendly to you, and in the end of the day, someone will invite you to stay in his house.

Remembering the warm hospitality I have so often received from Egyptians, I was left thinking about how different the experience was of Nepalese workers employed alongside Egyptians. Egyptians happily included me in their circle of mutual friendship and solidarity, but with workers from other countries they often made an effort to demonstrate how much better they were. I was treated well and welcomed by all largely thanks to my status as a white European—that is, a person with privilege. Being treated as an equal by a privileged person carries with it a sense of recognition, while being treated as an equal by another poor person in direct competition for status and space can be experienced as a challenge and a threat. This labor of distinction by oppressed people, aimed at feeling that they are better than other equally oppressed people, combined with the necessity to rely on people one can understand and trust in a difficult context, makes racist prejudice and dislike a prevalent mood among the poor and exploited workers in the Gulf.

Subaltern racism is not simply a coincidental side effect of labor migration. It is a functional part of the way countries like Qatar are governed. The guards told me that Qatar has a quota system that dictates how many guest workers are hired from certain countries while still maintaining an overall Muslim majority within the population as a whole.[13] In a similar manner, the company's workforce consisted of several nationalities whose relative numbers were also dictated by quota. From an organizational standpoint, such systematic plurality may appear dysfunctional. Many otherwise simple tasks were enormously complicated due to the lack of a common language. Given the communicative aspect of guard work, why not hire only Arabic speakers? The answer is that the number of Arabic speakers (or of any other ethnic or linguistic group for that matter) is intentionally restricted by the quota system in order to prevent the politicization of and collective action by workers. Up until the 1980s, there were many more Arab workers in the Gulf, but when Palestinian workers became mobilized in support of Iraq after the Iraqi occupation of Kuwait in 1990, many Palestinians were expelled, and it became policy within the Gulf states to have a low number of Arab workers coupled with a plurality of different, mutually hostile ethnic groups (Hanieh 2011).

Foreign residents make up more than 80 percent of Qatar's population (Schafenort 2014, 72). At the banks on Grand Hamad Street, practically all work, from the top levels of banking business to the bottom level of guards and cleaners, was performed by foreign nationals. Migrant domestic workers clean Qatari homes and nurse Qatari children; migrant construction workers build the streets and the houses. The entire infrastructure is maintained and guarded by migrant workers. The police and army comprise migrant workers, with the exception of the top levels of command. If migrants took a united stance, they could take possession of the entire State of Qatar in half an hour without firing a single shot. Of course, they will not. Because they hate and distrust each other much more than they will ever hate their employers and the system of exploitation on which the State of Qatar is built, it will never happen. The rulers and owners of the system have every reason to feel safe.

Subaltern racism is part of an architecture of power in which an entire society is systematically depoliticized and demobilized: migrants, because they would have much to lose and little to win from political instability and because they are divided by class and ethnic boundaries, and citizens, because the system provides them with a highly privileged status, even if they are not part of the ruling elites (Kanna 2010; Davidson 2014). But aside from making a revolution impossible, subaltern racism also has more immediate consequences for the workers, for the experiences they can gather and the dreams they can have. The channeling of solidarity and trust along ethnic lines also restricts the range of what is considered worth learning, knowing, imagining, and desiring. In a way that resonates with and reinforces the narrow circle of life marked by work sites and accommodations, subaltern racism is a power that guides a migrant worker's dreams toward a specific, narrow, circular path.

5

ENDURING AND RESISTING

The workers were critical of the system and aware of the extent of their exploitation. Lokraj told me:

> It's just like when the Europeans transported and sold Africans into slavery in America. What happened to the Africans then, happens to us now. We are transported here, the company sells us, commands us. There is no choice. In Nepal, we changed from a kingdom to a republic. If we could take action, if we could organize a strike, we could change this country.

Difficult as it was, the situation of the security guards was nevertheless better than that of many other workers. But they were stuck in a job paying just enough to make it worth the trip, unable to change to a better-paid job and with no legal possibilities to claim their rights or improve their working conditions. This generated a grave sense of injustice. Since there was little the workers could do to change their situation, they did as much as they could to manipulate it, in order to save money, make life more bearable, and take symbolic revenge for the exploitation they endured.

Workers such as Hamza, who took his job seriously and tried to excel at it, were seen by their colleagues as having an inappropriate working attitude. As Lokraj on one occasion reminded Hamza:

We could die for the company and they still wouldn't give us an extra reward. There is no use in making sacrifices for the company. We already work for them twelve hours a day, 365 days a year—that's sacrifice enough. That's why one must *khalli walli*.

Khalli walli is a rapid pronunciation of the Gulf Arabic phrase *khallih yiwalli*, literally meaning "let him tend to his own affairs" and idiomatically translatable as "never mind" or "who cares?" To *khalli walli* is to evade things, or, if it is not possible to evade them, to let them not hit one with too much force.

Sleeping at work, for instance, was a regular thing to do, especially during long daytime shifts. On Fridays when the bank was closed, the responsible supervisor would *khalli walli* and arrive at the bank only around noon, allowing the guards to sleep, since there was nothing to do anyway. The best sites to work were those where nobody was looking over one's shoulder and where one could socialize, play computer games, read, or take a nap. The worst sites to work were those where one was not allowed to sleep: night shifts where it was not tolerated by the inspectors, and high-security sites like the Central Bank, where there were rows of cameras surveilling the security guards.

The workers were involved in various little schemes to trick the system in order to save money and trouble. Because mobile phone calls were expensive, the guards had devised a way to cheat the phone company on phone bills. The former national monopolist Qtel offered a subscription with one thousand free minutes per month, payable at the end of the month. But if one left the country before the end of the month, the company couldn't claim the bill. Tawfiq's supervisor, Zayd, told me that several times he had taken a subscription in the name of someone who was leaving within a month and then called home as much as he wanted for a month. He told me, "They have been stealing from me for seven years now. I can steal a little from them, too."

Every loophole that could save money, effort, or stress was a small delight for the guards. They were outspoken about it and saw it as a way to retain a degree of dignity by being paid back, in a way, for at least some of the exploitation they had experienced. Such tactics of manipulating a system to one's own ends have been famously discussed by Michel de Certeau (1984) in his *The Practice of Everyday Life*. In order to understand social reality and relations of power, de Certeau argues, it is necessary to pay attention to the minuscule ways of doing things and "making do" under conditions one has no possibility to change. De Certeau's view of the tactics of the weak (as opposed to the strategies of the powerful) can be read as a counterpoint to Michel Foucault's (2007) analysis of discursive power and discipline: questions about the procedures and techniques of power beg questions about how the living deal with the condition of being subjected to biopower.

De Certeau's vision has a strongly emancipatory undertone in its search for sites where the weak can command some power, no matter how limited. However, the condition of the workers in Qatar compels me to be more pessimistic than de Certeau was. A tactic is a mode of action that takes its framework for granted: it is about making the best out of the situation while reckoning with the inevitable. The tricks and diversions involved in tactical actions are not necessarily subversive—in fact, they can be a constitutive part of the system itself. Personal networks, favors, exceptions, diversions, and tricks are not exceptions to a rule; rather, they are at the heart of the governance of the Gulf states (and others). The powerful and the weak alike make systematic use of them (see Osella and Osella 2012), but the weak have, by definition, less power to deploy such maneuvers in a way that might systematically improve their position. The way employment contractors prevent workers from organizing by hiring workers from various nationalities who distrust each other too much to take a common stance is a prime example of how a system of exploitation relies on the way the exploited make do with their situation. Of course, sleeping at work, working badly, and leaving bills unpaid are not directly profitable for the system in the way that subaltern racism is. But these actions do not challenge the system either. Rather, they give it a softer edge.

Some resistance is possible, however. At the end of my second week in Doha, the workers in one accommodation staged a protest action against the company. Shortly after moving to a new accommodation in the Nasr neighborhood (not its real name) of Doha, they were ordered to move again. The Egyptian guards refused. Hamza was one of them. He recounted to me what happened right after the events took place:

> We refused to move to a new accommodation today. We have a very nice accommodation. It's in a smart area near the palace of a prince, so the whole area is well kept, the air is good, it's a healthy place to live, and we have wireless internet. The company wants us to move to another housing. The Nepalese moved first. Then the Sri Lankans and Indians followed. But the Egyptians decided to stay. We have a good accommodation, and we are tired of being pushed to move every once in a while, transporting all our bags, the beds, and all the rest. Every time you move to a new accommodation, things get broken, somebody loses a bag, somebody loses a uniform. We want to stay where we are. And the new accommodation is large, with three floors and many nationalities together, and that always means trouble. Today is a very good day. It's the first time we've taken a positive stance.

The discussion took place during a cigarette break at the back of the Bank of Eastasia, in the company of Girgis, Sayf, and Lokraj, who lived in the same accommodation. Unsurprisingly, the company had threatened to fire the protesting workers. Girgis said that the threat did not deter him:

> Nasr is the cleanest and best accommodation, and we are going to stay, and if I'll have to go back to Egypt, that'll be fine with me.

I had first heard about this protest on the previous day. Tawfiq had predicted to me that the protesting workers would all be fired and sent back home. But now it looked like they were winning, since there was talk that the Egyptian workers from the accommodation where Tawfiq stayed (which was far worse than the one in Nasr) would move to the new accommodation as a way to rescue the company from losing face with the Nepalese, Sri Lankans, and Indians who had already agreed to move.

Hamza, Sayf, and Girgis appeared happy and proud of their ability to take a collective stance. Sayf raised his fist in a demonstration of their unity in the struggle. However, the struggle was not truly unified. All the Egyptians living in the Nasr accommodation refused to move, but the other nationalities had already left. Lokraj was among the Nepalese who had relocated from Nasr to the new accommodation. He admitted that conditions there were worse, with more than ten persons per room and only one bathroom per floor. Previously, Lokraj had shared with me his dream of collective action by the workers that might change the whole country. But ethnic segregation prevented him from participating in the small-scale show of resistance that was now taking place.

Some days later, Tawfiq and I walked to the Nasr accommodation to visit friends. It was indeed the best and most comfortable accommodation I had seen on my trip. Our hosts told us their protest had been successful because many of them occupied important functions and could not be quickly substituted by workers without appropriate training. This made a wholesale firing impossible. They also said they were so fed up that they no longer considered being fired and deported much of a loss. Because they were fed up, they could not be easily intimidated. Together, these factors made resistance possible and successful, albeit within a very limited framework.

The protest by the workers in the Nasr accommodation might seem insignificant compared to more dramatic instances of labor unrest at other times and in other places, including some labor actions in the Gulf states. But the very act of saying no and taking a united stance was indeed a rare occurrence. For those who took part in the refusal to move house, their show of resistance generated a sense of power and possibility. As our conversation shifted from the protest action to the men's general opinion of Qatar and their dreams for their own future, Sayf said, "On the question about what I think about this country, I say that it needs a workers' movement. It needs a workers' revolution." The experience had thus given some of the men involved new dreams. For some of them, it may even have contributed to their desire for political change upon their return to Egypt (Gruntz 2012b). For Tawfiq, it certainly had this effect, and I return to that part of his trajectory in Chapter 10. But back in Qatar, the collective action of fifty men neither crossed the ethnic divide inhibiting collective action nor forced any sustainable improvements in working conditions. No worker's movement was formed, and no workers' revolution broke out in Qatar.[14]

6

FAMILIES ONLY

On Fridays, industrial and construction workers spent their day off socializing with each other on Grand Hamad Street in the old part of downtown Doha. They were all from South or Southeast Asia and almost uniformly male. The bank guards worked seven days a week and thus did not join the gathering taking place directly in front of their work sites. Every available patch of shade on Grand Hamad Street was full of people soon after Friday prayers, and more people kept arriving over the course of the afternoon.

One block west of the northern end of Grand Hamad Street is Souq Waqif, an area of restaurants and shops that was recently rebuilt to resemble a historical market. Souq Waqif and the corniche are popular among Qatari citizens and well-off migrants. Those locations were off-limits to the workers who gathered on Grand Hamad Street. In the street dividing the two areas stood a line of guards and policemen who prohibited them from crossing the streets and occasionally ordered the workers further away from the street corners. On weekends (that is, Thursday evening and all day Friday), shopping malls and parks were for "families only." Although the corniche and Souq Waqif were not officially restricted to families on weekends, in practice the workers were not welcome there. The workers, although many of them are married and have children at home, are considered "bachelors," subject to a strict policy of segregation to prevent them from causing any harm or disturbance to "families" (Andrew Gardner 2012a). Native Qataris form a conservative and gender-segregated society, and there is great concern in Qatar about male workers looking at, photographing, speaking to, or in any other way disturbing Qataris and wealthy resident women. Sexual harassment in public is a punishable offense.

Of course, this system of segregation is not just about keeping lone men at a safe distance from families: it is also a means of keeping poor people at a safe distance from wealthy people.

Tawfiq and I used Fridays for outings, thanks to the leniency of his supervisors, who allowed him to leave his shift early. One Friday, we walked down Grand Hamad Street, passing through the crowds of workers and crossing the well-guarded street corner leading toward Souq Waqif and the corniche. The guards allowed us to pass without asking any questions. At the corniche, we boarded a bus bound for a shopping mall in Dafna, at the northern end of the corniche, where an area of skyscrapers was being constructed. The mall had a bus stop so that low-income workers could also reach it, but when we arrived at its entrance, a group of five people from the Philippines—two women and three men—were being denied access. Since it was a weekend, the mall was for "families only"; thus, the third man was one too many and was prohibited from entering. But the guards asked no questions when Tawfiq and I strolled past them and entered the mall. We walked around, bought tickets for the Doha Tribeca Film Festival beginning the following week, and by sunset, we were heading back toward the corniche. We took in the atmosphere there for a while, then walked slowly back in the direction of downtown Doha. Along the way we stopped and entered a park on the other side of the corniche road. The park was crowded with families. Again, because it was a weekend, the park was reserved for "families only." It was a distinctly feminine and family space, and we sensed we should not really be there. But we continued to walk around unmolested.

Although we were two men, with no women or children accompanying us, it was simple to walk past all controls into "families only" spaces, due to the color of my hair and skin. My looks associated me with the class of wealthy migrants (also known as "expats"). By accompanying me, Tawfiq was, by association, included in the expat class for whom a different set of rules applies. Souq Waqif and the corniche were built for people like me. I could enter a shopping mall on any day. (With the park, we were pushing the limit; we might have been asked to leave.)

Like all Gulf states, Qatar is a hierarchical and segregated society where citizenship, class, and ethnicity come together to create a complex system of privilege and exclusion (Davidson 2014; Hanieh 2011; Vora 2013; Kanna 2010). The logic of "families" and "bachelors" is part of this system. But it is not just about keeping native Qataris ("citizens" in the local jargon) apart from migrants ("residents"). This system is also a means of segregating migrants into two groups: those who earn an income sufficient to bring their families with them and those who cannot afford to do so. Furthermore, it segregates migrants of European origin from migrants of Asian and Middle Eastern origin. It is a form of segregation based on class and income, accentuated by racism.

Tawfiq happily seized the advantage that my position in this system offered him. The park was a pleasant place, a fine spot for a family outing. It had hills, curving paths, stairs, fountains, cafeterias, and playgrounds for children. Tawfiq enjoyed being in a place where many women were present. But it was meant to be only for families to enjoy, and in Qatar you can only have a family if you have money, due to the high cost of housing. Zayd, one of Tawfiq's two supervisors in the bank, was married, but his wife and children lived in Egypt and bringing them to Qatar was beyond his means. He told me that even a small apartment would cost at least 3,000 riyals per month—twice as much as his supervisor's salary. This is why one rarely sees children in the neighborhoods where low-income workers live.

As we strolled through the park, Tawfiq commented to me, "In this country, you need a woman, and you need money" *(al-balad di 'ayza wahda wi-'ayza filus)*. But in order to have a woman in Qatar, you need to have money—much more money than even a senior guard earns. If Tawfiq had had both money and a woman, he would not have migrated to Qatar in the first place.

The gendered and sexualized logic of class segregation produces different ways of being a migrant in Qatar. The segregation of "families" and "bachelors" distinguishes between those who can actually live a full life in Qatar and those who work and endure for the sake of a life located in Egypt, Nepal, India, or the Philippines.

Living as a male "bachelor" means living a homosocial life apart from a few, mainly formal contacts with female employees at the work site or in nearby businesses. This condition of enforced gender segregation, combined with a heteronormative culture of masculinity—where the potential erotic dimensions of men living together are suppressed or hidden—meant that the guards constantly talked about women and to a great extent defined their own position by criticizing the Gulf societies' sexual mores.

For women from the Egyptian bourgeois classes, Qatar and the Emirates can be actually rather comfortable places, since sexual harassment in public spaces is rare and the authorities exert significant effort in preventing its occurrence. While they would have to endure constant comments and occasional grabbing by men in the streets and other public places in Egypt, in the Gulf states women can walk along the corniche and stroll in shopping malls without fear of being annoyed or troubled,[15] and should trouble occur, the police are on their side. The male guards, by contrast, felt that they were deprived of the possibility of sweetening their daily life through flirtation.

As I was sitting one afternoon by the car park behind the Bank of Eastasia with Lokraj, Tawfiq, and Sayf, a Nepalese supervisor joined us for a smoke. A female bank employee, or perhaps a customer, walked by. The men watched her pass in silence. As soon as she was gone, the supervisor criticized the guards for not paying enough attention to her.

The supervisor: Why didn't you say to the lady who just passed that she is beautiful? Aren't you into women or what? You have to talk to the ladies and tell them they are beautiful, that they look good. Not the ones in *'abbaya* [that is, not the Qataris], but the others, yes. They want to hear it, it makes them happy.

Sayf, hesitantly: I may say that to the Filipina ladies, but not to others.

The supervisor: No, all the women want to hear it.

As we walked back to the Bank of Oceania, Tawfiq, who had kept silent, commented to me:

Talking to women can be dangerous here. He told us to go and talk to the lady, but why didn't he do it himself? He was afraid, too, and wanted to send us instead.

Yet while the workers were subject to strict policing by the Qatari state to contain their dangerous sexual energy, they usually saw themselves as more civilized and moral than the Qataris. Just before this discussion, Lokraj had told me about the many things he found strange in Qatar. The strangest thing for him was the position of women:

The people have their culture and I have mine, and I let them be as they are, but still I find it very strange here with women. They have to walk all veiled, and one man can marry four women—four! But the women can only marry one. I find that very strange.

Also the Egyptian guards, most of whom were Muslims and agreed with polygyny and covering dress for women, sometimes described Qatari sexual mores and gender relations as strange and inferior to their own. Before my visit in Qatar, I was already aware of the way some Egyptians present themselves as followers of a moderate middle path between what they see as licentious Westerners, who lack moral limits, and Gulf Arabs, whom they view as hypocrites who preach conservative values but act like animals. What struck me in Qatar, however, was that several Egyptian men explicitly described themselves as romantic and "cultivated"[16] in contrast to their stereotypical depiction of Qatari men.

One occasion when this topic came up was on the evening of Tawfiq's and my visit to Amr at his work place at the Eurasian Sports Association. After his shift ended, Amr suggested that we walk to his accommodation instead of taking the company minibus. He led us directly into the Family Park, a large park that was "families only" every day. He knew the park well because he had been posted there before he was transferred to the Sports Association. It was late in the evening, and the park was filling with people arriving there to enjoy the cool night air. Soon after entering, we were stopped by a guard who politely told us that the park was for families only. There were three of us, and this time my looks were of no help. But Amr showed his company badge. Since the park was policed by the same company they worked for, we received a collegial greeting and continued on our way.

As we walked over an artificial hill, Amr quietly pointed at a couple, dressed in traditional Qatari white and black, leaning on each other. As we walked further, he told us:

> Although this is a family park, it's also full of lovers. As a guard I got to see a lot of things . . . And that's a big problem here. They have built these malls and parks, and now the people who are in love come and exploit them. But here it's wrong, because it's contrary to their customs. Here they apply Islamic law to the full extent. You know, in Egypt it would be natural. In Egypt if a park were called a "family park," everybody would know that it's the lovers' park. Although as an Oriental (*sharqi*) man, I would also be worried about someone going to the park with my sister. But still, romance and couples going to the parks are natural (*tabi'a*) in Egypt, it's the way it is. But here, they are very strict about women. And the women here are very hot. They are full of desire, but the men are cold. They don't have the culture of romance and flirting. . . . Here, the husbands are not romantic toward their wives. When the Qatari man is in bed with his wife, he just gets on top of her and, tik-tik-tik, he does it quickly, leaving his wife hot and unsatis-

fied. They don't have the same sense of romance as Egyptians have. That's why they say here about Egyptian men: Just a look by you can make a woman pregnant.

Amr went on telling anecdotes about the many compromising things he had witnessed in the park. Citing his words, I do not mean to say that he offered us a truthful description about love and sex in Qatar. He did not. How would he know how Qataris actually make love? Rather, Amr tells us how Egyptian workers perceived and imagined Qatari intimacy and society from their position within it. He seamlessly wove prejudice and rumor together with observation (see also Andrew Gardner 2012a), and in doing so, he sketched an idealized image of the cultivated, romantic, and irresistible masculinity that distinguishes Egyptian men from others (in the perception of Egyptian men, that is). Finally, he entertained us with erotic anecdotes that were in much demand among men longing for contact with women.

Many other Muslim Egyptians are rather more inspired by the strict gender segregation and religiously inspired mores of the Gulf. Migration circuits between Egypt and the Gulf played an important role in the 1970s Islamic revival in Egypt—an issue to which I return in Chapter 13—but as Lucille Gruntz (2012a) shows in her research on Egyptian return migrants between the 1970s and the present, many also develop a sharpened nationalist identity in contradistinction to Gulf mores. Since the labor regime in the Gulf is strongly gendered and sexualized, the ways in which migrants distinguish themselves from (or also search for inclusion in) Gulf societies are gendered and sexualized as well.

But more than labor regime and nationalist identity are at work in making the intersections of migrant labor, gender, and sexuality so prominent. The entire project of labor migration is propelled by gender and sexuality. Men are working in menial jobs such as security personnel, in a place like Qatar, either because they need to save money to start a family or because they already have a family to support. In order to do so, they need to live in the enforced state of a less-than-real life, which troubles their sense of manliness—the same manliness which they are expected to prove and establish by being capable earners who can return home with a nest egg. This leads us to two key issues at the heart of the nexus of migration and dreams: money and marriage.

7

EVERYTHING CIRCLES
AROUND MONEY HERE

Although many of Tawfiq's colleagues appreciated the flashy consumer spaces, conspicuous consumption, and abundant wealth that Qatar and the other Gulf states display, I also often heard variations of the lament that the entire country of Qatar is an artificial simulation where the only thing that matters is money. Tawfiq's description of Villaggio Mall as reminiscent of *The Truman Show* (in Chapter 1) is one variation of this lament. Another was presented by Bhupal, a guard from Nepal who manned the reception desk in the Bank of Oceania. One day he showed me photos of the mountains and green valleys in Nepal on his mobile phone, saying:

> I don't like this place. Everything circles around money here. And it is all desert, no green. In Nepal, everything is green, in the spring you see all the flowers on the fields and the green forests, and on the horizon you see white mountains. Nepal is a poor country, as you know. That's why I am here. What else can I do? But there, even the poorest people have good, fresh food. Even if someone is very poor, he has a garden and sells vegetables from the garden at the market. The vegetables are fresh, directly from the garden. The milk is fresh, directly from the buffalo. Here, they sell milk that stays good for ten days. The food here is artificial and full of chemicals. The people here say that just three hours after eating they feel hungry. They feel hungry all the time because the food here has no power. You eat, but you stay hungry. If you rub the chicken they sell here between your fingers, it turns into dust.

Bhupal linked the artificial and unreal nature of Qatar with the prevalence of money, which is the driving force of everything. This is a complaint I heard repeatedly from guards, from both Egypt and Nepal: money ruled over everything, and the meaning of life was reduced to making, saving, and spending money.

During one of the many discussions that I witnessed about whether Qatar is a good or a bad place and whether Qataris are respectable people or not, Girgis pointed out:

> Today at my work, two guys were debating. One found the Gulf good and another found it bad. The first one earns 10,000 riyals, the other 1,000.

The claim that "everything circles around money here" is more than mere critique. It is a recognition of the reality of workers' existence in Qatar. In their lives in particular, everything really does circle around money.

How much money people earn was a recurring topic in discussions. Nobody found it indiscreet to ask, "How much money do you earn here?" One evening, as we walked to the small supermarket near the accommodation to buy soft drinks, Tawfiq's roommate Ali asked me:

> Ali: Why don't you come to work here? You could make so much money here!
>
> Samuli: Why would I? I have a good job in Germany that gives me reasonable pay, and I have a good life.
>
> Ali: How much do you earn?
>
> Samuli: About 2,000 euros. In purchasing power, it would equal perhaps 7,000 riyals here.
>
> Ali: But here you could get many times more. There are people in the bank who get 20,000, 60,000, even more than 100,000 riyals! You could get any job or start a company, buy a villa and a big car and get a lot of money. Many Europeans come here for the good money. And Europeans get three times the salary of Egyptians.

I replied to Ali that I wouldn't change my good life in Berlin for the lifestyle in Qatar for all money in the world, but he wasn't convinced:

> Ali: But you could work here a couple of years to save money and then go back.
>   Samuli: They would be lost years of life. I have seen so many migrants who never return because they depend on the income and get used to a standard of living.

Ali, however, had observed that when Europeans come to work in Qatar, the first thing they do is buy a Hummer. He remained unconvinced about why I would not want to live in Qatar, although I would enjoy amazing privileges, such as triple the salary for the same work.

That labor migration is all about money seems obvious, to say the least. If it weren't for the money, none of the Egyptian and Nepalese men I met would have been in Qatar. But the way in which a calculating logic of incomes, expenses, and savings dominated their lives and discussions stands in remarkable contrast to daily life in Egypt, where issues of money are discussed discreetly and where people do not constantly talk about money, although it is a constant concern in their lives. It also stands in contrast to the way young men would tell me about their motivations to migrate. Of course, money was an important—usually the most important—motivation to travel. But it was usually discussed in parallel with the complementary desire to gather experience, to have a more exciting life, to enjoy a greater degree of freedom, and to have rights (Schielke 2015, 158–60). Furthermore, the money that the young men dreamed of was seldom described in terms of exact figures, of profits and losses. Instead, the men would speak more vaguely of the "fortune" *(tharwa)* that one would gather through hard work in a few years and then return home with to "build a life."

The reality of migrant work narrows down the imaginative margins of freedom, excitement, and making a fortune to a calculus of income and expenses—a question about how much money one can save this month, whether one will be able to save enough in the course of one's contract, and whether one should extend one's contract. One seldom earns as much as one hoped. The conditions of work and life are harsher than anticipated, the cost of living higher, and the labor regime more oppressive than the men could have imagined before leaving. Whatever dreams a worker may have are located in a different place and time. Here, while at work in the "dystopia," as Tawfiq called it, everything circles around money—because money is what they are here for, because it is so difficult to have enough of it, and because there are others who have it in abundance.

This is an ambivalent experience. Money is existential power: it makes things possible. Having money means having freedom and choice. And in a place so thoroughly and explicitly commercialized as Qatar, one learns to understand money as the only conceivable form of power. What cannot be calculated in cash becomes hard to imagine, as revealed by Ali's bewilderment over my insistence that I would not wish to live in Qatar. And yet the workers were constantly complaining to me that they were not free and had no choice, that instead of living and acting of their own accord, they were mere slaves.

8

THINGS MONEY MUST BUY

According to Georg Simmel's (1989) classic treatise, money creates freedom by making people's relationships of interdependence complex, abstract, and invisible, thus producing many freedoms but at the same time making social bonds weaker. Following Simmel, money creates choice, but also alienation.

In contrast to Simmel's thesis, the migrant workers suffered from alienation, yet they did not feel that they were compensated for their alienation with more choice. They could not choose to look for another job because of the *kafala* system. Their range of choices was reduced to a binary opposition between working until the end of their contracts or returning home empty-handed. Most importantly, they had little choice about what to spend their money on once they had it.

Bill Maurer (2006) argues that money is often far less abstract than in Simmel's vision because it is linked with specific morals and purposes, specific things one needs to buy with money. This is also the case with the money migrant workers earn. Far from being an abstract source of choice, migrant money is deeply purpose-bound and also strongly gendered (Andrew Gardner 2012b).

One afternoon, Tawfiq came to pick me up at the coffee shop where I was writing up my field notes and told me, "Let's go to the money exchange." It was his payday. We went to the cash machine of the bank where he had his account. He had 1,144 riyals in his account, and he withdrew 1,100. He would have taken it all out, but the machine did not give notes smaller than 50. With the money in his pocket, we walked to a nearby commercial area catering mainly to migrant workers, entering the office of a Western Union agent equipped with a number of desks that handled transfers to different countries. At the desk for transfers to Egypt, Tawfiq handed over his customer card and ID and made a transfer to his uncle of LE1,500 (approximately 190 euros at the time). With the fees (which were moderate, 15 riyals) the total cost was 1,023 riyals. Tawfiq was left with 77 riyals for the rest of the month. He kept no savings with him. He sent all the money he could save to his uncle, who administered his savings. The uncle, in turn, passed on the money to Tawfiq's mother. Most of it was used to construct a new story for their small house in the village (that new story would eventually become the apartment into which Tawfiq and his wife would move after their marriage). In other months, Tawfiq sent less. Usually he first had to pay his debts to the grocery where he bought his food. But the shop had gone out of business, and he had no debts to pay this time. The previous month he had sent nothing because he had spent all his money on presents, which he sent with me to his family. He told me that he felt guilty about sending no money the previous month, which is why he sent almost all of his salary this time—as quickly as possible before he could spend it. He said he could borrow some money to manage until the end of the month, adding that "nobody dies of hunger here."

During his two years in Qatar, Tawfiq bought two things for himself: a laptop and a cell phone. The rest of the money went toward presents for his family, supporting his mother, and the construction of the addition to his family's home. In the last two tasks, he was not alone. The first two floors of the house had been built mainly with money sent by his sister, who worked as a nurse in Saudi Arabia. Tawfiq's close family owns no land and they have no connections to secure a well-paid job in Egypt's extremely nepotistic labor market. In order to build, to marry, indeed to do anything that goes beyond subsistence, the most feasible path available to him and his sister was working abroad.

Perhaps Tawfiq might have been able to make some money in Egypt, although he did not believe so, explaining to me on more than one occasion before leaving for Qatar that "the only investment that brings profit in Egypt is leaving the country." In any case, he had little choice over what to spend his money on. After his original plans of using Qatar as a stepping stone for migrating to the West had proved unrealistic, he was left with no other options than making the best out of his situation and saving as much money as he could to "build a life" (*yibni hayah*), to "form himself" (*yikawwin nafsuh*), and, eventually, to "gain stability" (*yistaqirr*)—all conventional Egyptian expressions for a man gaining the resources necessary to marry and care for his family.

Building a life is not something one can do as one wishes. While there is a variety of available paths to becoming a grown-up man (Ghannam 2013), they mostly share a conventional series of necessary steps a man must take. Practically all these steps relate in one way or another to marriage.

On one of the few occasions when Tawfiq and I sat in a café in central Doha to meet his friends and colleagues—a luxury he probably wouldn't have indulged in if it hadn't been for my visit—we were joined by his colleague, Abdelwahhab. Abdelwahhab hadn't shaved for days, which revealed that he was no longer working (guards on duty had to appear to work cleanly shaved). He said he had quit a few days earlier following a conflict at work. Now he was waiting for his paperwork to be completed so he could leave. He did not tell us what exactly had happened, but he was fed up. And it was not just the company or the *kafala* system he was fed up with; he was fed up with Arab society.

He spoke at length, addressing me much of the time:

What exactly is it that you are after in your research? The hopes, aspirations, and frustrations of each one of us? The individual ideas of everyone are different, and people from the city and the countryside have different life contexts, different costs and standards of living and housing that they can hardly catch up with . . . [He elaborated to me what buying an apartment costs in Egyptian cities, and why renting is not a good option.] But the thing in common that pushes everybody in Egypt to migrate is the need to get married, and the cost involved. A young man of twenty-one in Egypt can nowadays expect to get married after he is over thirty because of all the expenses involved in every single step, from the engagement to the wedding ring to the apartment to the dower to the wedding. The problem is that every step takes money. I'm engaged. But that is only one step, and I have more and more expensive steps ahead. Money for marriage is the single thing that everybody must be after. There is no choice. In Europe, it's different, it's not necessary for people to get married, or you can live together without being married, and people are not so preoccupied with offspring as they are in the Arab countries *(al-watan al-'arabi)*, where everything circles around begetting children. And not just any child: it has to be a boy, not a girl. Maybe very religious people can accept it as a will of God when a girl is born, but otherwise people are upset—unlike in Europe, where people are happy about a child, boy or girl; they are not so preoccupied about maintaining the male line. And you may marry, you may live together without marrying, you may have children or not—you have choices. Here in the Arab countries, you do not have a choice.

Don't think that I say it just because I have seen it in American films. I have learned a lot here from contact with the Filipinos, the Thais, the Germans, the Americans; all the different people, each with their different way of life. I have very good Filipino friends and I like their ways, although they can be very different from ours. And also for me it is difficult to move beyond my way of thinking to understand them. Among us, for example, it would be very difficult to be friends with a man or a woman who is gay. In Europe it may be more normal, but in the Arab world it would make friendship very difficult if you know that someone is gay.

Here, very few people think about such questions. When I go back to Egypt and try to talk with them, they will not get you, they will say, "What are you talking about?" All they care about is smoking hashish, following football, watching television—an Arab, Hollywood, or Hindi film—anything but politics. Or they talk about politics in a useless way that leads nowhere. You are lucky if you find one in a thousand who makes something productive with his mind.

Abdelwahhab's point of view is unusual insofar as he emphasized how much he had learned from the strange yet interesting ways of other people working in Qatar. It is unusual also in that he questioned the principle of offspring—especially male offspring—which is such a highly held value and a crucial measure of manhood and womanhood in Egypt and the Arab world. Living in Qatar had given him a wider range of dreams but fewer practical means to pursue them; he still faced the necessity of following the prescribed path laid out for him.

Most other young men were explicitly sympathetic toward the conventional path of social becoming. It was their taken-for-granted, obvious dream, which is why they seldom took the pains to explain and analyze it the way Abdelwahhab had. They were often critical of the conditions, but seldom of the project itself. However, regardless of how they positioned themselves toward it, they all experienced the same necessity.

In Egypt (as in most of the Arab world) marriage is prohibitively expensive, and the groom is responsible for the greater part of the expenses, including the dower and presents, the apartment and the fur-niture, and a wedding party. Marriage is usually the largest investment in a man's life. At the same time, marriage is considered inevitable and necessary—remaining unmarried and without children is widely seen as a terrible failure. Therefore, almost everybody spends enormous energy on getting married—whether they are enthusiastic about it or not, content with the conditions or unhappy with them—and this comes in spite of them knowing that they may well end up marrying somebody with whom they will be unhappy. All this is further complicated by the high cost of marriage, driven further upward because, at least in rural locations, migrant workers can offer more money and better material conditions than most non-migrants can. After all, this is the purpose of migrant money.

The metaphorical and material steps on the path to building a conventional life are part of what Ghassan Hage (2005) has called "existential mobility"; that is, the sense of being able to move forward in one's life. However, this movement is often not an end in itself. The steps one needs to take in order to become a man in the full social and moral sense of the word are expected to lead one toward an ideal condition of relative non-movement: stability *(istiqrar)*. In her ethnographic study of an Egyptian steel plant, Dina Makram-Ebeid (2012) has shown how a public-sector enterprise and its workers relied on two distinct but related senses of stability: first, stability in the political sense of a predictable, controlled condition of affairs, and second, stability as a moral ideal of masculine becoming whereby a "stable" or "settled" *(mustaqirr)* man is able to take care of his family and fulfill his community obligations, independent of the help of others, while being able to support relatives and friends in need (for a comparative case, see also Gaibazzi 2015a).

The aim of migrant money is directed toward such moral ends and is thus the opposite of alienation. But the conditions of making that money are often alienating and unsettling. Hence, the workers complained to me about both their feelings of alienation and their lack of choice.

And once one actually does get married, this condition does not end. Instead, it becomes perpetuated when men who now become fathers need to rely on work abroad over an extended period of time to support their families back home. The moral purpose of money as a means to build and to maintain a family is associated with permanence. But money is not permanent: it only exists so long as it is replenished by revenues.

9

DREAMING OF THE INEVITABLE

During Tawfiq's and my visit to the Nasr accommodation where the protest action had taken place (see Chapter 5), a discussion evolved among the men sharing the room about whether coming to work in Qatar had been worth it or not and what their preferred destination would have been. One of them, Rizq, said he had would have preferred to go to Europe rather than the Gulf. In fact, he had already boarded a bus to Libya with the intention of making his way to Italy by boat when he heard the news that dozens of migrants attempting the Mediterranean passage had just drowned in a shipwreck. He got off the bus and returned home, settling for the Gulf as a safer option. Safe but meager, as he pointed out, "Here we also get just enough to live." This provoked his roommate Sayf, who had worked as a French teacher in Egypt before coming to Qatar, to say:

> Yes, we are alive, praise to God, but do we live? Do we really live here?! This is not a life!

A debate then occurred between Sayf and Rizq about how much purpose there was in going through long periods of hardship in Doha. Rizq was optimistic that it would be worth it. Sayf was skeptical, however:

> The problem is that there is no alternative. In Egypt, if you want to realize something, if you want to build a life, you need money and

that compels people to migrate. But it fails here. Here, I haven't been able to realize what I wanted; on the contrary, I have moved backward. I haven't been able to realize anything on a material plane, but at least I have gained experience.

Sayf told us that he had arrived with bags full of books rather than clothes. He came here to find better work but was now stuck in a menial guard's job for two or three years. Rizq disagreed: "We all knew the work we came here for." Sayf insisted, though:

> People don't know what it means to be in the Gulf. All they know is that there is money in the Gulf. So if you come here, people expect you to stay for a while and come back with money. But the reality is different. While we are here we miss many better opportunities that we might have seized in Egypt. But you can't return immediately. If you return early, people say, "You're not a man, you bring bad luck" (*fi wishak faqr*). So we try to endure a year, two years, three years. My parents don't know what work I do here. All they know is that I work in a bank, but the pay is bad.

Throughout the world, there is enormous pressure to put one's faith in the reality of the dream that migration will bring quick wealth, and migrants everywhere abide under an equally enormous pressure to confirm that dream.[17] Young men who have never migrated but dream of doing so often experience their present condition as one of boring, frustrating nothingness: an empty state of waiting, where migration appears as *the* path out of nothingness into productive being (Graw 2012; see also Elliot 2015 on women who have to wait). To tell a young man in an Egyptian village not to dream of migration is like telling him not to hope. How could one not believe in the dream of migration, facing the undeniable reality that marriages are arranged and that houses are built using the money migrants have earned?

The pressure of hope makes communication about the migratory experience difficult. It is common for Egyptian parents not to know the kind of work their sons do abroad (with daughters, they are more eager to know). The part of migrant workers' lives that family and friends at home are likely to know is their occasional returns home on holiday, or at the end of their contracts.[18] On these occasions, migrants are under pressure to perform their success through generous spending, presents, and fashionable clothes, no matter what the circumstances of their return might be. Many proverbs and songs relate the hardship and homesickness of migrants. Critical media reports occasionally describe spectacular cases of injustice Egyptians abroad have faced (Cantini and Gruntz 2010). But telling about one's personal hardship and working conditions is more difficult. Migrants often don't want their parents and families to worry—and they want to appear successful in the eyes of their peers and potential brides. When they do try to describe the difficult sides of their experience abroad, they often find that people either fail to believe them or lack interest.[19] A migrant talking about bad pay and difficult conditions may also be suspected of trying to hide the wealth he has accumulated. A part of this suspicion is justified. Just as some migrants return with a great display of success but empty pockets, others come back complaining that the trip hardly paid for the day-to-day expenses and yet some years later they build a new house with the money they had secretly saved. Egypt is one of many societies that rely heavily on migrants' remittances but where most people know little about how migrants actually work. The price of migrant money is known in general terms but is less spoken of when it comes to individual experience.

The men gathered in the room in the Nasr accommodation were perfectly aware of this. They told me that they would not—could not—repeat at home what they were telling me and each other. They would play their part in fulfilling a dream that was projected upon them—a dream which they, in turn, would pass on to others. They would get married with the money they earned, they would embody the image of success expected from them, and in doing so they would compel others to follow in their footsteps. They would leave it to the songs and proverbs—and to anthropologists—to tell what the price of that dream was.

But they would never question the principle of having a dream. Over and again, I was told that one needed to have a dream to keep going. During the discussion in the Nasr accommodation, Sayf echoed this sentiment, pointing out that despite the many setbacks,

> one has to keep up hope. Our sublime and exalted Lord *(rabbina subhanahu wa-ta'ala)* tells us that he sends some to paradise and some to hell. Why does he do that? He created us to have hope. There is no life without hope, without dreams.

Dreams are an ambiguous matter: they give us direction; console us; motivate us; keep us alive. Michael Jackson (2011, xii) has argued that the sense that "there is more to life than what exists for us in the here and now" is probably universally constitutive of a meaningful life. Dreams and hope arise out of an excess of human imagination and energy that keep us striving for more than we need for basic survival, for other, better things than what are immediately available. But one cannot dream freely and at will. Some dreams are extremely compelling to pursue, while others can be difficult to entertain in the first place. Furthermore, just as dreams provide openings beyond the here and now, they also direct one toward specific ends. To complicate things even more, we may not even know beforehand what those ends will be. With his theological framing of hope as part of God's plan, Sayf reminds us that while there is indeed no living without the productive excess of dreaming, we nevertheless cannot realize our dreams at will.

One way to think about the complex and ambiguous power of dreams is to look separately at their powers to reproduce the limits of the expected, on the one hand, and to open up paths that may go beyond these limits, on the other. The purpose of labor migration from the point of view of most migrants and their families is to realize a conventional, conservative life of material comfort within intact networks of family and community. Additionally, migration may also involve dreams that exceed the conventional framework of socially recognized aspirations. As Abdelwahhab's critical reflection about Arab family values demonstrated, the experience of working abroad often gives both kinds of dreams richer contours and a greater sense of urgency. But the exploitative conditions of migrant work, especially at the low level of salaries received by Doha's bank guards, make it difficult to actively pursue anything other than the conservative ideal of social reproduction. The situation may be more balanced among migrants in the well-paid sectors (Vora 2013), but among lower-income migrants, the experience of migration can reduce the range of imagined possibilities that one can reasonably pursue.

The expectations invested in migration are a prime example of the productivity of "imagination as a social practice" (Appadurai 1996, 31), even an instituting ground of society (Castoriadis 1987). However, aspirational dreams are not simply freely available. Some are more available, compelling, and textured than others. And the pursuit of dreams has material consequences. The limits and borders that prospective and actual migrant workers face are not only of a material–economic kind: they are also borders delimiting the imagination. The aspirational dream of quick wealth and lasting success through migration is propelled by returning migrants, who feel compelled to act according to its dictates. Yet it does not prepare men for the reality of migrant life. And some aspirational dreams can become so powerful that they sideline others.

Being a migrant worker teaches one to dream differently than one did before migration. Dreams of quick wealth, travel, leading an interesting life, or overcoming the boredom of daily life often give way to a monotonous and boring existence that is felt to be less than real, dominated by the aim of saving enough money to return home, where a life to be built awaits. Being a migrant worker teaches one to dream in numbers, to calculate in a prudential fashion, measuring the value of one's days by the balance of one's bank account: to desire, in short, the things that can be purchased over those that money cannot buy. It also teaches one to suffer and to endure in pursuit of those inevitable dreams that can only be realized with the help of money.

By *inevitable dreams*, I mean aspirational projects and imaginaries that are both realizable on a material plane and socially and morally recognized and encouraged. Strictly speaking, they are highly compelling rather than inevitable, but in my fieldwork experience, they did appear inevitable from the point of view of most of the people who pursued them. This is *the first power of imagination* involved in migratory work: the power of dreams that are so compelling that their pursuit takes on the subjectively experienced power of inevitability. One may not succeed in realizing them, but one definitely will try. That power makes the pursuit of other dreams less likely, even if the means to pursue them might seem to exist on a material plane.[20]

This is not to say that migrants do not gain anything in terms of what Arjun Appadurai (2013) has called the capacity to aspire and what Pierre Bourdieu (1984) describes as social capital, and what I call the scale and texture of dreams. They certainly do. Money earned abroad provides the capacity to act, the ability to do and make something in one's life. Working and living abroad is likely to provide one with an imaginative capacity that has more texture and scale in terms of skills, social networks, and general experience. However, that capacity is limited by an oppressive labor regime, and it is guided toward specific ends by the conventional shape of social becoming and by the calculating logic that does not support the pursuit of things that cannot be bought with money.

The limiting nature of this first power of imagination should not be mistaken as something negative or inauthentic. It is not enforced upon those who pursue such dreams against their will. On the contrary, most young people in the Arab world strive for marriage and conventional stability with conviction and determination (Schwarz 2017). It is also not a destructive power. Limitations are productive. They do not simply obstruct; they also guide. They compel great numbers of people worldwide to focus their efforts on specific projects. The first power of imagination, the power of inevitable dreams, is extremely productive—albeit often in contradictory ways.

In Chapters 13 and 14, I return to the open-ended and unsettling consequences of the migratory experience by looking at the shaping of imaginaries and trajectories of class mobility and religious devotion among Egyptians. For the time being, I only want to point out that the first power of imagination—the inevitability of certain imagined, socially sanctioned goals—does not simply reproduce the given and the conventional. Its consequences are more complex. Labor migration reinforces the values and institutions of a conservative society—kinship bonds, houses that keep the male line of a family together,[21] arranged marriages, wealth, religion—but it does so in a way that may at the same time unsettle and transform them.

In a materialist, Marxist analysis, this power might also be called the "relations of production," but my point is that relations of production are also always relations of imagination. When it comes to earning money to build a house, get married, and raise children, the arenas of economy, morality, and dreaming are inseparable. This inseparability is what renders the first power of imagination so effective, capable of producing and reproducing undeniable and compelling realities. And yet this power has probably always coexisted with another, weaker power: that of the desire for something more than what is known and what can be expected, a dream to have other dreams.[22]

10

TO HAVE OTHER DREAMS

The idea that a daring dream can change the world is prominent in the Gulf states, where the promotional language that surrounds prestige projects speaks of the imagination as the only limit, while authoritarian politics celebrates the figure of a visionary leader for whom nothing is impossible (Kanna 2010; Wippel et al. 2014). In the spirit of trickle-down economics, neoliberal developmental strategies of empowerment also promise that poor people can change their situation for the better by daring and learning to have other dreams. For the security guards working in Doha, however, many things were not only impossible to realize but also difficult to dream of.

It is exceedingly difficult to pursue other dreams. To start with, it is not obvious to even have them in the first place. Imagination relies on an available stock of knowledge, figures of speech and ways to think, popular culture, underlying and explicit moral sentiments, and intuitive limits of the possible and thinkable. Most of the time, people do not think up dreams from scratch but construct them out of an existing stock of known ideas and conventional aspirations. Some of these combinations can be highly original and innovative, but the needed materials and the possibilities to cultivate one's skill in combining them are not unlimited, nor are they freely available. "Other dreams" should thus not be mistaken for authentic ones, as opposed to a socially imposed first power of imagination. Almost all aspirational dreams are made up of socially available stuff. What makes some dreams difficult to achieve is not where they come from but the scarcity of the means to realize them, their lack of social acceptability, and the low likelihood of their success.

Nevertheless, Tawfiq has been struggling hard to create a space in his life to nurture and to pursue other dreams than those inevitable ones provided by the first power of imagination. His limited success in doing so is telling of what this second power of imagination can and cannot accomplish.

During the two years he spent in Qatar, Tawfiq's main allies in this struggle were poetry and novels. He read a great deal of literature and wrote a number of poems describing a sense of longing for the beloved, the home village, and the homeland, about sleepless nights and estrangement mixed with a determined search for something real and true. Some of the prose and poetry he read was highly political. On one evening we spent together in the accommodation, he introduced me to a poem called *The Last Words of Spartacus*, written in 1962 by the Egyptian poet Amal Dunqul. A disturbing evocation of tragic resistance, it appeared to me as timely as ever when Tawfiq recited a passage as we sat together on the carpet of the cramped room:

> Do not dream of a happy world
> For behind every emperor who dies is a new emperor
> And behind every revolutionary who dies is helpless sorrow
> and a tear in vain!
> (Dunqul 2005, 91–97, my translation)

With its dark, pessimistic tone, the poem was well suited to a time when Egyptians anticipated that President Hosni Mubarak's son Gamal would soon succeed him in office. And yet for Tawfiq the poem expressed not resignation but resistance. Reading it in that place and time was a way of not accepting the status quo; rather, it was an incitement to dream of a happier world in spite of its apparent impossibility.

Tawfiq's immediate struggles at that moment were more mundane. He was of two minds about whether he should stay longer in Qatar or return to Egypt. He had saved only a little money, and back home his meager civil servant's income from the local health center could hardly cover life expenses. It is hard to resist the prospect of an ongoing monthly salary, even if one knows that by staying one may miss other, better opportunities. The salary is a solid reality, while these other opportunities are not. For this reason, most guards stayed for three to five years instead of two, and some stayed for many more years, although the pay was bad.

Tawfiq returned from Qatar exactly two years after his departure, without extending his contract. Back in Egypt in late 2010, he told me that he had read Paulo Coelho's novel *The Alchemist* in Arabic translation (Coelho 1996) several times during his time in Doha. This novel in particular, he told me, gave him the strength to return and try his luck elsewhere.

The Alchemist is an explicitly symbolic parable, a story of the winding paths taken toward the fulfillment of a dream and a plea for a life of individual self-realization guided by one's unique, true potential. *The Alchemist* can be read as utopian literature for the neoliberal era, congruent with the spirit of entrepreneurial individualism. Read in that context, it is not a radical work at all. But for Tawfiq, it was radical reading matter, providing an imaginative ground to think of a life that was not reduced to the closed circle of migrant money—a life that may have surprises to offer. If the reading of a novel could be powerful enough to help a person act against the compelling power to stay a little longer, then this raises a question about the power of dreams not only to create paths so compelling that other paths become almost impossible but also to suggest alternative paths despite their apparent impossibility.

The years that followed can be read as an attempt to balance these two powers in Tawfiq's life.

Not long after his return to Egypt, Tawfiq was looking for a new contract to work abroad. On January 24, 2011, he traveled to Cairo for an appointment with a labor agent the following day. He never had that appointment, because the next day turned out to be the first day of the January 25 revolution: Tawfiq joined the protests in downtown Cairo. In the months that followed, he became involved in a leftist revolutionary group in his village. They organized clean-up campaigns and political meetings, drawing much attention in the village but failing in the end to alter local politics (Shehata and Schielke 2013). After having been a very unmotivated worker during his time in Doha, Tawfiq was transformed into an energetic and capable political activist, more patient and persistent than many of his comrades, who were easily frustrated and demotivated by setbacks. Perhaps patience and persistence were among the things he had learned during his first migration.

Later, political setbacks turned into defeats, and defeats turned into a full-scale counter-revolution, followed by the establishment of a new authoritarian regime. But in the spring of 2011, it seemed that one could very well dream of a happy world, that resistance was useful, and that things could change for the better. This was still the prevailing mood in May 2011 when Tawfiq left for a new two-year contract as a security guard in Abu Dhabi. Revolution or not, his salary in the health center was bad, the Egyptian economy was at a standstill, and he needed money to get married more urgently than ever. But this time, something more was going on. He was in love.

Like many Egyptian lovers these days, Tawfiq and Zarqaa first met online. Her brother is a good friend of Tawfiq, but Tawfiq and Zarqaa were not officially introduced to each other until the summer of 2012, when Tawfiq returned to Egypt on a vacation. He paid a visit to Zarqaa's parents, who live in a neighboring village, asking for her hand from her father. It was a match of the sort much desired yet difficult to realize in Egypt: a match where love and marriage are united.

In Egypt, as in most of the Arab world, romantic love has a powerful cultural heritage and presence in poetry, on television, in films, in conversations, and on social media alike (Strohmenger 1996; Menin 2012; Fortier et al. 2016; Jyrkiäinen 2019). But Egypt is also a conservative, patriarchal society where gender segregation, women's subordination to men, and the primacy of family and parental interests are held in high esteem. More often than not, the power of love is weaker than the powers of class, money, family allegiances, and religious sensibilities concerning gendered modesty—not to mention the fact that in actual practice, love often takes possessive and violent forms.

The dream of a shared life based on romantic commitment is not unconventional—on the contrary, it is widely present and quite conventional in Egyptian society. The often harsh conditions that prevail in actual marriage arrangements make that dream only more attractive and compelling. And yet it lacks the self-reinforcing dynamics of the first power of imagination that propels the union of migrant money and conventional marriage. Love is a possible dream, while marriage is an inevitable one. Marrying the person one loves is risky, difficult, and at times plain illusory. Migrant money plays an ambiguous role in the process (Gruntz and Pagès El-Karoui 2013).

Although migrant money has given young men a more independent position with regard to their parents' will in deciding whom to marry, it remains closely tied to interest-based family-arranged marriages. Returning migrants can offer better material conditions than suitors lacking such funds.[23] Young women may be able to refuse a suitor, but the wealthier the suitor, the more difficult it is to resist. However, migrant money can also be a way to turn a romantic attachment into a successful marriage proposal, and many prospective couples pin their hopes on such a detour. It is a risky path, as the waiting period can be long and in the meantime either the prospective bride or groom may be compelled to give in to family pressure, accepting an economically more attractive partner. Many are the stories of men who returned to find that the woman they loved had already married—and of women who patiently waited only to see that after finally returning from abroad, the man they loved married his cousin.

Against these odds, Tawfiq and Zarqaa made it. In the autumn of 2013, they joyfully celebrated their wedding, moving into a small apartment in his mother's house, built and furnished with money he had earned in Qatar and Abu Dhabi.

Tawfiq told me that his time in Abu Dhabi had been better than his time in Qatar. Thanks to the clear aim he had this time—marrying Zarqaa—it was a less frustrating and confusing experience than Qatar had been. And thanks to his experience in Qatar, he had been careful to find a contract with a company paying double the salary he had received in Qatar. Still, he had barely made it. Tawfiq's savings could provide little more than a shadow of Gulf-inspired up-market lifestyles. Unlike more well-off migrants, who erected new houses plotted on agricultural land, Tawfiq and his wife's apartment was built atop his mother's house, on a plot of land measuring approximately twenty-five meters square, located in the old village center. Limited as his means were, the marriage might have been delayed or not taken place at all if it had not been for the shared determination and insistence of Tawfiq and Zarqaa, and the supportive attitude of Zarqaa's father, who took a generous stance toward Tawfiq's material obligations in the marriage arrangement.

Tawfiq's ability to turn the money he earned in Abu Dhabi into a marriage with the woman he loved and who loved him was a solid victory of the second, weaker power of unrealistic dreaming. But it was not a victory of a durable kind. Being poor and lacking resources means being exposed to trouble from all sides. Following Michel de Certeau's (1984) terminology, one can make tactical moves and seize opportunities as they come, but it takes a safe base and a position of power to strategize. And no matter what its motivations and prehistory may be, marriage means becoming involved in a complex network of family and social relationships, some of which are supportive while others bring conflict and stress. It means expectations, responsibilities, roles to fulfill, and bills to pay.

When I met Tawfiq and Zarqaa again early in 2014, the joy they had radiated at their wedding had been replaced by a subdued and serious mood. They had planned that both of them would contribute to the family household through their work.[24] But Zarqaa had not yet finished her studies. For the time being, responsibility for the family's income weighed entirely on Tawfiq's shoulders. Immediately after his wedding to Zarqaa, he had been of two minds whether he should remain in the village or try to save more money by extending his contract in Abu Dhabi. In the end, he had no choice. His contract in Abu Dhabi had been canceled for political reasons. Fearing that the political turmoil in Egypt could reach its own territory, the United Arab Emirates had systematically denied security clearance renewals for all Egyptian employees in the security sector. Now he had to find a way to make ends meet in Egypt.

11

A BIGGER PRISON

What the second, weaker power of imagination can accomplish under favorable conditions is to change the way a person perceives the world and thus to change that person's range of possible paths of action. But for Tawfiq, the conditions have been far from favorable. Every step forward has been followed by new formidable obstacles that either hindered him or pushed him in another direction. Unlike the protagonist in Coelho's *The Alchemist*, who returns to the start of his path to find the treasure he pursued all along, in the world where Tawfiq lives there is no final happy arrival, only ups and downs in an ongoing struggle.

Tawfiq has many times reflected with me about this experience through the image of walls.

In 2007, I asked him whether he would return if he could leave Egypt. He replied, "If you were released from a prison, would you go back?" Two years later in Doha, over lunch one afternoon in a Palestinian fast-food joint, I remembered our conversation and asked him how he saw it today. He replied:

> It turned out to be a bigger prison. The problem is how to know the borders of your prison. It's a prison of many walls. After crossing one wall, you find another wall. It's like in the beginning, you're in the innermost circle. And when you jump the wall, you find yourself only in the next circle of the prison. You have to know where the borders of your prison are so that you know how to jump all

the way over the outermost wall. But how to know which wall is the outermost? That's the problem.

Tawfiq's reply was a philosophical reflection on the condition of people who try to find openings in a world where what presents itself as an opening only leads to the next prison yard. This was what working in Qatar felt like for him and his colleagues. Having realized the long-desired chance of *safar* (travel), they found themselves in a situation where the possibilities for action and movement were circumscribed, although in a different way than had been the case before their migration. This image of concentric prison walls kept me busy over the coming years.

In spring 2014, as we sat in Tawfiq's freshly furnished, although very small, living room and he told me about his experience of the two and a half years he spent in the United Arab Emirates, I remembered it again. I asked how he saw it now that he was married and had returned from his second contract abroad. This time, he developed a different idea:

> In the area where we worked, they have laid out plantations where they grow palm trees and keep camels and other animals. The plantations are enclosed in walls. When you go down a road, it is often surrounded by such plantations from both sides, so you move between two walls. The walls are there not so that the animals can't get out: they are there so that you can't get in!

Tawfiq drew a map depicting a road with an arrow showing one's direction of movement, two walled plantations on either side, and another arrow showing the direction of movement prevented by these walls. Thinking about walls as a metaphor for limitations, Tawfiq evoked them not simply as barriers that hinder one but also as guides that direct one along the road laid out for you.

But as soon as Tawfiq was done with his drawing, he presented another, different thought about walls:

There is always a wall. Getting married was a wall I needed to jump over, and as I overcame it, I face the next wall of raising children and building a future for them. Life is made up of a series of walls that one needs to jump over. There is always a wall to jump over.

These different metaphors show varying aspects of the inherent limitations to what one can imagine, pursue, and realize.

First, there are *walls that hide other walls*, evoking the way all aspirations, plans, and trajectories only have a certain range and are always limited by greater powers and structural inequalities. Such walls are not only a hindrance—they also motivate one to overcome them. And since such walls impede a view of what lies beyond them, they invite one to focus on the immediate hindrance in the hope that afterward everything will be easier. International borders and visa regimes often work in this way: the difficulty of crossing the border gives that which lies beyond the imaginary contours of paradise. Only after reaching the other side will one learn the restrictions and troubles that are awaiting.

Second, there are *walls that guide* one along a path already laid out in advance, reminding us that limits are also productive, enabling movement in certain directions while impeding others. This is an apt representation of the linkage between migration, social reproduction, and the political economy of oil. At their most effective, such limitations are successfully normalized and naturalized so that people exposed to such walls may not want to cross them in the first place, instead focusing their efforts toward progress along a laid-out path. And yet the fact that this is only one of three images of walls proposed by Tawfiq reminds us that the naturalization of available, limited paths does not always succeed.

Finally, there are the *walls that one always needs to jump over*, indicating that struggle, and perhaps also transgression, is inseparable from living. Walls-as-thresholds might thus be considered not so much as a hindrance to social becoming but as one necessary aspect of the process: the ability to cross them is what makes one an adult. And unlike in the first image, there is no outermost wall, only an ongoing struggle to over-come one threshold after another.

The image of walls that require one to jump over them echoes Yassin al-Haj Saleh's (2017) argument that freedom is fundamentally transgressive: an act of going out *(khuruj)* from and also against the taken for granted. In fact, Tawfiq considers himself a seeker of free-dom, and yet his successful acts of *khuruj* (going out) appear less radical than that envisioned by al-Haj Saleh. Rather, they seem to combine elements of conformity and transgression in a way that resonates with Paola Abenante's (2015) argument about "limits of discourse." Abenante tries to understand situations where some people find that their ways to aspire, act, and think reach their limits and do not help them. In such situations, they may be compelled to search for "hermeneutic openings," ways to rethink and rearticulate the way their conditions and actions are constituted and conceived. Tawfiq's experience of migration has brought him often to such limits, and at times he has consciously searched for openings of the kind Abenante evokes. His meditation about walls sug-gests that limits and openings are interdependent, and that life is an ongoing struggle structured by limits that direct and guide, as well as by openings that are themselves limited. I find Michael Jackson's (2011) idea of "life within limits" an especially good concept for thinking about such struggles and about how one may take some limits for granted, strive to enforce others as ethical guidelines, and seek to manipulate, transgress, or overcome others.

Late one evening in November 2014, one year after his wedding and five years after my visit to Doha, Tawfiq and I took a walk around his home village. Before we met, he had announced to me that he had a lot to tell, yet now he was silent.

We sat down in a humble café comprising a few chairs set along an irrigation canal. Until recently, the other side had consisted of fields where rice was grown in summer and alfalfa in winter. Now the fields were disappearing beneath a row of new houses in various stages of construction: some were still concrete and brick skeletons, while others were already inhabited. After tea and a cigarette, Tawfiq started to speak. He had more worries than he could handle. There were unsolved conflicts with some of his relatives; problems with Zarqaa's first pregnancy had resulted early on in a miscarriage. And she had had to repeat the final year of university, forcing her to commute to the provincial capital almost daily, a round trip of four hours. And then, he added, there were all the material problems. Everything cost money. Education and transportation cost money and so did doctors' visits. High inflation made prices rise faster than his civil servant's income.[25] And as a health inspector, he could not make a side income by selling private services the way doctors, teachers, or policemen could. As a consequence, Tawfiq had to stretch every penny: "If I buy a bad pack of cigarettes, it's a sacrifice to buy a new one." He said that due to all these worries and pressures,

> I haven't opened a book and I haven't written since I got married. I have a pile of books I want to read, and I would have a lot of time, too, but it feels like from having too much time, I have no time. And problems don't come one by one so that you can solve them step by step. They pile up all at once and create pressure, and they leave you no peace of mind to read and write.

He saw only one solution: going abroad again for another contract of two or three years: "If I were working in the Gulf, I would make LE5,000 [approximately 560 euros at the time] per month, and all these material crises wouldn't happen." But this time, that option was exceedingly difficult.

In 2013 and 2014, Gulf states expelled hundreds of thousands of migrant workers in an attempt to increase the number of citizens in the active workforce.[26] At the same time, the Egyptian economy was stagnating. The hopes Tawfiq and many others had invested in the revolution had been replaced by deep frustration. All those things that had once seemed possible now appeared further away than ever. The vision of a different Egypt that he and his friends had struggled for in the spring of 2011 had been marginalized by a confrontation between Islamist movements, on the one hand, and the heavy-handed military regime that tolerated no critical voices, on the other. Nor could the regime deliver the economic prosperity it had promised. Not that there was no money in Egypt. Between 2011 and 2013, Egypt experienced a tremendous construction boom facilitated by the temporary absence of government controls, which made it cheap to build houses (no need to pay bribes), further motivated by a prevailing sense of insecurity that made building houses appear like the safest investment for one's savings. As result, within a short time huge amounts of private capital were being invested in housing. Now the houses were standing in the outskirts of villages and cities, often half-finished, and little money was available to invest in production or trade. At the same time, the Egyptian state had raised LE64 billion (over 7 billion euros at the time) through selling bonds for an expansion of the Suez Canal. The expansion, opened in 2015 and officially dubbed "the new Suez Canal," was a highly publicized prestige project that has so far failed to realize the promised increase in revenue.[27] In the short term, the project even created additional bottlenecks. It put the Egyptian pound under pressure against foreign reserves, and the canal bonds attracted local capital that might have been invested in other sectors of the economy.

As result of all these factors, there was enormous pressure to search for work abroad. People from privileged classes and highly qualified sectors could hope to study in Europe or to get a well-paid job in the Gulf. Poor people like Tawfiq had fewer options. Tawfiq said that a few weeks earlier he had traveled to the city of Beni Suef—a trip of several hundred kilometers—to pursue a possible job offer in Saudi Arabia, despite having doubts about the offer. So many people had shown up to apply that Tawfiq could not even get inside the labor agent's office.

Tawfiq was ambivalent about the new houses across the canal. On the one hand, he saw them as a wasted investment that resulted in a great deal of money being bound up in houses instead of creating jobs. On the other hand, the houses were material proof that there was still money to be earned—and that the place to earn it was abroad. Pondering this, he repeated what he had once said to me eight years earlier: "In this place, the only worthwhile investment is an investment in travel *(safar)*."

As a migrant worker in Qatar and later in Abu Dhabi, Tawfiq had been working toward something in the future, a dream to realize. With the emotional and material hardship he faced, and with some of his dreams remaining beyond reach while others pressed upon him, he was often depressed and frustrated. But eventually his migrations did help him to realize the conventional dream of starting a family and building a life. Against the odds, they also helped him to realize a less likely dream: marrying a woman he loved. Extending some of his energy to paths like love, political commitment, and literature, he was able to create some little openings, some precarious paths for other dreams. But now he faced the iron pressure of political economy and the responsibilities of a married man. In this moment, what other dream could he possibly pursue than that of finding yet another contract in the Gulf?

12

UNTIL THE END OF OIL

Aspirational projects of becoming and transformation—be they moral, religious, political, economic, or some other kind—are productive in an open-ended way. They often produce something else than what was initially promised and expected. This is not simply a matter of success or failure.

One of the paradoxical outcomes of the pursuit of the dream of a better life through migratory work is that the migrants' success in making money makes it more difficult to return to the stable life one hoped to build.

Among those who stayed longer in Doha were the supervisors Zayd and Antar, Tawfiq's immediate bosses at the Bank of Oceania. Both were married with children, their families residing in Egypt while they lived and worked in Qatar.

On one of my last days in Doha in 2009, I encountered the supervisor Zayd outside the bank, speaking on the phone with his son in Egypt. After the phone call, he was visibly moved. He told me:

> I'm sick and tired here. I'm sick and tired here. I want to go home so much. But I can't return yet. What will I live on? I will have to hold on for one more year.

At this point, Zayd had been in Qatar for seven years. He had married with the money he earned there, and his family now lived from his income. The last I heard of him, in spring 2015, he was still in Qatar: his late father had lived for decades as a migrant worker in Qatar as well.

The double alienation migrant workers experience—alienated work combined with alienation from the life they work so hard to build—is emotionally stressful. Migrant workers usually hope to return home as quickly as possible—many have told me that they will return home after just one more year. But after that year, usually yet another year of *ghurba* (strangerhood) abroad awaits them.

The following day, I again met Zayd and the other supervisor Antar at the bank, and I asked them whether they really were going back to Egypt soon. They answered: "We will be here until the last riyal. Until the oil runs out."

This is a fitting description of the perhaps most unsettling outcome of labor migration: the need to postpone the beginning of that good, stable life toward which one works so hard. The attempt to turn one's dreams into reality through migratory labor means, in practice, that one has to endure a less-than-real life while waiting for real life to begin. And one often has to do so over extended periods of time: for just one more year, until the end of oil.

At the lower income levels (that is, in the vast majority of jobs available in the Gulf), salaries are calibrated to be just a little bit better than what one could earn at home. For this reason, different nationalities receive different wages. The money is usually less than hoped for, but there is some. So long as it flows, returning for good would mean a return to nothingness—"back to point zero," as Amr put it when he was considering whether to extend his contract or to return home. And yet sooner or later, migrants to the Gulf do return. But it is seldom a return for good.

In March 2015, Tawfiq and I went to visit Hilal, one of his former colleagues in the company, who lived in a village not far from Nazlat al-Rayyis. After five years in Qatar, Hilal had returned to Egypt in October 2013. We met him in his women's clothing shop. With the help of business connections made in Qatar, he had gained access to occasional deliveries of imported clothing. These were the backbone of his business. He told us that the most important benefit of his having worked abroad was social: the people he became acquainted with, the connections he had made, and the ability to make use of these. Thanks to these connections made in Qatar, he was able now to make a living in Egypt.

The networks and knowledge necessary for trade are among the most useful and sustainable forms of experience one can gain from migration to the Gulf (see Osella and Osella 2012; Pelican 2014; Marsden 2016; Stephan-Emmrich 2017), and the social profit of migration in combination with trade is one instance of the sort of open-ended imagination that makes things happen—a mastery of practical knowledge that allows one to realize dreams. But still, the knowledge and connections Hilal commanded were scarcely enough. He stood at the bottom of the global hierarchy of traders. His connections were limited, his profits meager. The income from the shop did not even properly provide for his family, and Hilal was, in fact, currently searching for a new contract abroad. Tawfiq told him that everybody who had been working with him either in Qatar or in Abu Dhabi were now again looking for work abroad.

Urgently looking for a new contract but not finding one, Tawfiq was getting worried that he soon might become too old for short-term labor contracts. He had just read the first draft of the Arabic edition of this book. Commenting on the passage about enduring until the end of oil, he said, "It's not an individual condition, it's the condition of the entire society."

For individuals, *ghurba* (strangerhood) is often a temporary stage in their lives. But enduring for one more year until the end of oil has become the condition of living for entire societies. Because workers are not allowed to settle permanently in the Gulf, migrating there creates a life of perpetual short-term *ghurba*. And therein lies a key to the unsettling potential of migrant labor for low-income workers. The unsettling effect of migration as a project to build a better life at home is not caused by its failure. If migration indeed brought no profits, migrant workers would not succeed in building houses and financing marriages. The pressure to migrate would cease. What makes migrant work unsettling is its marginal success, providing enough to keep one working, building, and modestly dreaming. But there is no treasure buried under a tree at the end of the quest.

Tawfiq spent three years looking for his next contract abroad. During this time, his daughter was born. In spring 2017, he finally departed for his third contract abroad, this time as a customer service agent in the United Arab Emirates. The salary was lower than that of a security guard, but it was the best he could get. His wife and daughter stayed behind in the village. For Zarqaa, Tawfiq's ongoing absence has been a painful yet also empowering experience, forcing upon her new responsibilities which she took on willingly. In spring 2018, Tawfiq returned home for his first one-month vacation. Around the same time, construction began on his new house in the fields outside Nazlat al-Rayyis. That house is a dream Tawfiq has had since before his marriage. With the money from his third contract, he could finally begin turning it into brick and concrete. In spring 2019, he extended his contract for two more years.

Back in 2009, to describe his and his colleagues' condition, Tawfiq had quoted a line of poetry by the Egyptian poet Salah Jahin (1930–86). It is based on the image of a traditional Egyptian water wheel, powered by an animal bound to the wheel and pushing it in an endless loop.

> Bull, shake off your blinders and refuse to walk in circle
> Break the gears of the water wheel . . . Curse and spit
> The bull: Just one more step . . . and one more step
> Until I reach the end of the trail, or the well dries up
> How strange! (Jahin 2002, 23, my translation)

The image of the bull and the water wheel unsettles attempts to understand migration through a binary ontology of movement and stasis, for a loop is a movement that keeps one in place. By citing the poem, Tawfiq described his condition but also wondered what might be done to change it. Until today, he has not given up on the hope that different possible paths, even a different world, may be possible. He is critically aware of the loop into which migrant work has thrown him. Yet at the same time he has learned well how to be a productive part of the migrant labor engine. He has thereby accomplished many of the conventional markers of adulthood. Along with millions of others, he keeps the wheel of oil-based wealth turning.

The figure of the water wheel is a poetic hyperbole, however. As much as the strivings and struggles of migrant workers resemble a loop, it is not a loop that brings them back to precisely the same spot. Rather, it can be better understood as a dialectic, a productive contradiction. Through the Gulf migratory loop, Tawfiq has accomplished many of the conventional markers of adulthood. But the life he has built is different in outline and details from the adulthood his father and grandfathers dreamed of or accomplished.

13

NORMALITY AND EXCESS

B y virtue of the first power of imagination, labor migration is a conservative aspirational project. It is spirited by a dream of normality, of a "life worthy of humans" *(hayat bani adamin)* in material and moral comfort. In that sense, labor migration to the Gulf appears as a normalization engine, a process that reinforces conventional moral strivings and naturalizes social and economic hierarchies.

And yet like the water wheel, the engine metaphor is also a hyperbole and therefore misleading if taken literally. Unlike in popular anglophone readings of Michel Foucault, where discourses often appear miraculously successful in producing what they promote, in my fieldwork I have gained the impression that such projects of normalization are powerful and productive in ways that may ultimately unsettle their initial aims.

International migration has undeniably transformed Egypt, to the degree that one cannot understand Egyptian society today as separate from the Gulf and other destinations for Egyptian migration. The Egyptian economy is, to a great extent,reliant on migrants' remittances.[28] Investors from the Gulf own large parts of Egypt's economy and real estate. The Egyptian state is economically and politically dependent on the Gulf monarchies.[29]

Labor migration also shapes the imaginary horizon of entire societies. Among the poor and the well-off alike, migration has become a global source of worldly optimism and a path to prosperity unmatched by others. In Egypt, it has allowed Gulf-inspired lifestyles to become deeply rooted among the wealthy and middle classes, and to be a compelling aspiration among the poor.[30] Migrations have also contributed to spiritual transformations in various religious traditions around the world (a point to which I return in the next chapter).

The dream of comfortable housing has taken material shape in reinforced concrete and red brick, changing the faces of cities and villages beyond recognition. In a matter of forty years, since President Anwar Sadat abolished travel and currency restrictions in 1974 and paved the way for Egyptians' mass international migration, Egyptian villages have been transformed from tightly knit communities of small mud-brick houses into semi-urbanized concentrations of large, multi-story buildings of red brick and concrete that sprawl into the surrounding agricultural land, providing greater connectivity with the wider world and a greater degree of privacy from the communal life of the village than had previously existed (Weyland 1993; Abaza 2013; Schielke 2015; Giangrande and De Bonis 2018).

The dream of marriage and offspring has transformed itself into expensive marriage arrangements, wedding parties, furniture and household items, and, most importantly, family lives that, in a paradoxical manner, reinforce and undermine patriarchal family ideals. They reinforce them when entire families depend on male migrants' money, which strengthens the values of family-arranged marriage and male guardianship. At the same time, lives built through migration undermine family ideals when migrant money bestows upon sons more independence from fathers and makes it more likely for newlywed couples to live in an apartment of their own, separately from the extended family. Furthermore, male migrants often end up living for a major part of their lives away from the home and family they struggled to build (Weyland 1993; Gruntz and Pagès El-Karoui 2013).

In spring 2017, shortly after Tawfiq left for his third contract abroad, his old friend Abbas returned to the village on vacation after working in Kuwait for four and a half years. He had found a reasonably good job as a clerk in a perfume store. He told me that his living conditions were better than those of most Egyptian migrants because he preferred to pay slightly more for housing. Instead of living in a cramped room, he shared a small apartment with two Christian Egyptians (because he liked their attitude, he said), and he did not feel that he was deprived of basic life comforts. Now he was back in the village, a successful man, freshly engaged and ready to be married.

In the years before his *safar* (travel), I had known him as a young man with many ambitions but few clues as to how he might realize them. Now he appeared transformed. He radiated confidence, knew what he wanted, and constantly spoke in numbers: what this and that plot of land cost, how much these or those construction materials cost, how much a wedding party costs.

His greatest pride was the house he had recently built—not with his hands, but with his money, since he had been in Kuwait while it was being built. It stood on agricultural land on the outskirts of the village where many other new houses were also being built. He showed me around, relating to me his design choices. We sat on the roof (which would one day be the floor on a new story) to smoke and enjoy the view over the fields. Knowing how much he had struggled as a student in Cairo before his years working in Kuwait, I was happy to see him now as the owner of a new house and hopefully soon a married man. For him, the trip had certainly paid off.

But the trip was not over. He was about to leave again for Kuwait in two days' time and would only return in the summer of the following year for the wedding party. Then, he told me, his plan was to live another four years in Kuwait, together with his future wife, who hopefully would be able to find work to contribute to the cost of housing. His long-term plan is to move with his future family to Cairo. If all goes well, the house in the village will stand empty except during holidays. Eventually, Abbas intends to sell the house at a profit and buy an apartment in Cairo.

Empty houses built by international and rural–urban migrants in their regions of origin are a worldwide phenomenon.[31] Each one of them tells the story of a dream of a rooted, conservative life in material comfort that has partially become unsettled by virtue of its own success.

Bringing one's wife along to the Gulf transforms a man from a *mughtarib* (migrant), living as a stranger in a strange place, into somebody who can actually have a full life abroad. The high cost of housing in the Gulf makes women's salaried work there more likely and attractive, and it contributes to subtly different household relations from those promoted by the ideal of a family life centered around a patriarch breadwinner. The house Abbas built was an inevitable dream, but it was also the material and financial foundation of a surplus or excess of anticipation, of the sort that made it possible for him not only to fantasize about a grander urban way of life but also to realistically pursue it.

When I met Abbas in February 2017, I gave him as a present a copy of the Arabic-language version of this book, which had just been released under the title *Hatta yantahi al-naft* (Until the End of Oil) (Schielke 2017), translated by Amr Khairy. I was traveling between Cairo, Alexandria, and the village, partly doing fieldwork and partly on a promotional tour for the book. In the end, doing promotion for the book turned out to be a form of fieldwork as well. Themes that came up in my encounter with Abbas also came up in discussions at book readings.

I gave three readings in 2016 and 2017, before and after the release of the Arabic book. At all these events, a majority of the people present had either grown up or worked in Arab Gulf states. Most of them had lived there as well-paid employees or the children of them. By virtue of the social milieu in which these events took place, they were mainly involved in or close to liberal-leftist intellectual circles. Although their lives in the Gulf had usually been more comfortable due to their class affiliation, they recognized their own experience in the trajectories of Tawfiq, his friends, and his colleagues. Because of the positions they had occupied in the class hierarchy of the Gulf, however, they focused more on their experience of upward social mobility.

At a reading in Alexandria in 2017, Khaled, a man in his twenties from the nearby industrial town of Kafr al-Dawwar who had grown up in the Gulf, commented that for his parents, who came from the lower middle classes, migration had been a conscious project of "upward movement in class" *(tatallu' tabaqi)*—a project that for his parents was one of improving material conditions and returning to their native small town, but from which he had gained a more cosmopolitan horizon of expectations. At a 2016 reading in Cairo, a man in his twenties said that he belonged to a class and generation of people who attended international schools in the Gulf and had been socialized into "the global bourgeoisie" *(al-burjuwaziya al-'alamiya)*, with the tastes in music, political views, and aspirations common to this class.

After 2011, Egypt witnessed the short but intensive flourishing of a vibrant independent cultural scene, often associated or openly allied with one current or another of the revolutionary movement. Parallel to my work for this book, the Alexandrian novelist Mukhtar Shehata and I conducted fieldwork in that scene for a research project on literary writing (Schielke and Shehata 2016). Notably, many of our interlocutors in that scene had grown up in the Gulf and returned to Egypt at the onset of adulthood. Empowered by the social and economic capital they and their families had accumulated abroad, they perceived the country that was now their home—Egypt—with a mixture of intimacy and estrangement. However, they represented not the mainstream but rather what may be called the bohemian fringes of the affluent bourgeois milieu. Social mobility due to high-income migration does not generally translate into alternative visions of life. Eman, a medical professional who had lived as a teenager in Saudi Arabia and as a young adult in Kuwait, and who in 2014 and 2015 participated in a writing workshop in Alexandria, described herself as a social misfit compared to her classmates, who almost without exception lived conventional lives as mothers and wives surrounded by material comfort.

Joining the global bourgeoisie is not a path Tawfiq and Zarqaa can likely attain, nor does it seem easily available for their daughter. But it is also not impossible. Some people from his extended family have been able to jump the social ladder. In a highly unequal society like Egypt, migration often reproduces social inequalities; yet it is also a feasible if difficult path of social mobility. And some of its imaginative effects become tangible in the next generation.

Thinking about migration, class, and ideals of the good life together suggests that the first power of imagination—the power of dreams to call for their realization—is not a closed loop, at least not under the present conditions of economic growth and transnational mobility. Imagination is a finite excess of the known, a limited, yet not fully contained margin grounded in our ability to anticipate more than the here and now. When people succeed in turning dreams into things and skills, this in turn can also generate new horizons, desires, and dreams that exceed the scope of the original dream. While other dreams are by definition weak, difficult to pursue, and unlikely to be realized, success in the realization of some inevitable dreams can transform certain unlikely dreams into compelling possibilities.

While I was promoting the book to Egyptian readers, another migration wave was gaining momentum. Not only people like Tawfiq and Hilal were urgently looking for contracts abroad in order to make ends meet. People who lived in relative material comfort were also searching for ways to leave Egypt. Before 2011, many Egyptians I met wanted to migrate temporarily, but fewer thought of leaving their homeland for good. Many of the latter were Christians skeptical about their future in an Egypt dominated by the religious sensibilities of the Muslim majority. And while previously migration had been something mostly men spoke about, I was now hearing from people of both sexes, of different social classes and moral and ideological stances, and from

Muslims and Christians alike that they were anxious to leave Egypt for good and to build a life abroad.

Partially this was related to the uncertain and oppressive conditions in Egypt after the counter-revolution. It became more difficult than before to be optimistic that one's hard work and savings abroad (or, in terms of upper-class migration, one's educational accomplishments and professional experience) would eventually constitute the basis for a viable life in Egypt. And yet in the past, things had been bad, perhaps far worse for many people. There had been other periods of great oppression, uncertainty, and crisis—but these had not been accompanied by a comparable generalized striving to look elsewhere to find the means to live a good, decent "life worthy of humans." The widespread urge to leave Egypt after 2013 thus appeared only partially a consequence of the difficult situation in Egypt. For another part, it was a consequence of possible better situations elsewhere having become not only compelling but also virtually and actually within the reach of increasingly many Egyptians.

The dream of young men from low-income backgrounds of a vaster, more exciting world of opportunities, one where a fortune waits to be grabbed by them, is fantastic in the sense that it does not include the practical details necessary to its fulfillment—details to which dreamers from provincial areas often have little access (Appadurai 2013). Their experience of *safar* (travel), *ghurba* (strangerhood), and circular migration teaches them skills and gives them knowledge of details that are mainly useful for continuing on the path of striving they have entered. People from more privileged milieus are more likely to possess the means to pursue a wider variety of paths and to take what one Egyptian migrant in Sweden once described to me as "bohemian decisions": choices that are not driven by the moral–economic calculus of saving money for inevitable dreams or making ends meet in the short term to survive. And yet migrants at the bottom of the class ladder learn things that point beyond the realistically attainable, and some of those things may transform into skills that open new possible paths. Abdelwahhab's critique of the Arab obsession with offspring; Tawfiq's willingness to take the risk of early return from his first contract, as well as his engagement in the revolutionary movement and his marriage with Zarqaa; Hilal's ability to turn some of the contacts he made into a trade network; and Abbas's plans for conjugal life abroad—all these stories testify to the potential of the circular path of normality becoming unsettled.

14

ESTRANGEMENT AND FAITH

Migration is a major source of this worldly optimism. But what about optimism that exceeds this world? The worldwide intensification of migratory movement often goes hand in hand with the hope for salvation and reward by God in life after death. And as people move from one place to another, they often also begin to approach their traditions of worship and ethics in new ways.

Some paths of travel are motivated by the desire to live a properly pious life in a land of true faith (Stephan-Emmrich and Mirzoev 2016). The risks and opportunities involved in migration often make both migrants and their potential brides highly aware of destiny, God's unknown plan that humans fulfill (Gaibazzi 2015b; Elliot and Menin 2018). Money, too, is far from godless: Arabic-speaking Muslims and Christians alike regard worldly income as a sustenance *(rizq)* from God, something which humans need to work for but ultimately do not earn solely through their own effort (Nevola 2015). In undocumented migrations across the Mediterranean, death is a tangible possibility and a reminder of the afterlife (Pandolfo 2007). The issue most debated among Egyptians, however, concerns the impact that migration to the Gulf has on how Egyptians understand a good life in material, ethical, and spiritual terms.

This issue arose at all three of the book readings I gave in 2016 and 2017. Some people in the audiences addressed what they saw as the destructive spiritual impact of the Gulf (especially Saudi Arabia). In their view, migration to the Gulf has transformed Egypt's once pluralistic, moderate, and solidarity-oriented society into a religiously conservative, intolerant, and fiercely materialistic one. This is a long-standing topos in liberal-left urban circles in Egypt.[32] It is a stereotype, insofar as it assigns responsibility (or outright blame) to the Gulf monarchies as external agents who have installed inauthentic, foreign mores and ideas in Egyptian society. And yet it does tell about a societal experience: migration has changed Egypt, and not only in material terms.

The rise of the Islamic revival in Egypt since the 1970s was concurrent with the policies of economic liberalization that also marked the onset of mass labor migration to the Gulf and Saudi Arabia. The Islamic revival was to a great extent accompanied by a theological shift from Sufi-oriented communal traditions with their focus on saintly and prophetic mediation and divine protection, to Salafi and other reformist-oriented movements that emphasize ritual purity, strict monotheism, and forms of ethical discipline dominated by the prospect of reward or punishment in the afterworld. This is also the kind of theology promoted by most Gulf monarchies (Oman, which follows a branch of Shia Islam, being an exception). And yet the idea that Saudi Arabia and other Gulf states simply exported their understanding of Islam by indoctrinating migrant workers does not quite resonate with my fieldwork experience and what I know about the history of the Islamic revival and comparable spiritual transformations in other religious traditions.

Saudi and other Gulf donors have spent much money funding mosques and promoting religious teachings close to their own. Saudi Arabia's role as the guardian of Mecca and Medina gives its religious institutions an unparalleled authority. Even so, the Islamic revival in Egypt is not simply a foreign import. In his work on Ansar al-Sunna al-Muhammadiya, Egypt's oldest Salafi organization, Aaron Rock-Singer (2019) argues that Egyptian Salafis at the onset of the Islamic revival enjoyed a significant degree of theological independence in relation to their Saudi allies. The Muslim Brotherhood (which shares with

Salafi and other reformist theologies the striving for clear identitarian boundaries, moral reform, and purified practice but has its own distinct doctrine, organization, and leadership) was founded in Egypt, from where it spread to become an international political and religious movement. Sheikh Abdelhamid Kishk (1933–96; see Hirschkind 2006, 58–59), whose cassette-tape sermons were instrumental to the Islamic revival in the 1970s and 1980s, was Egyptian and preached in Egypt. Sheikh Muhammad al-Qaradawi, a scholar close to the Muslim Brotherhood, migrated from Egypt to Qatar, where he became a globally influential religious authority (Gräf and Skovgaard-Petersen 2009). Egypt has thus been a major exporter rather than just a receiver of reformist theologies and Islamic revivalist movements.

But that does not yet explain the simultaneous rise of the Islamic revival, economic liberalization, mass migration, and Gulf-inspired lifestyles (Tsourapas 2017; for comparative cases, see Osella and Osella 2007; Stephan-Emmrich and Mirzoev 2016). The experiences and expectations of a migrant's life seem to provide a significant opening for new religious movements that highlight individual moral discipline, ritual purity, closure against religious others, cosmopolitan connectedness through shared faith, and an intense and anxious preoccupation with reward and salvation that resonates with the logic of wealth and profit— all key characteristics of the Islamic revival, especially its reformist varieties (Schielke 2015, 124–27). However, the role of the Gulf may be more of a catalyst than an active proselytizer. A life in narrow circles of solidarity and distrust aligns well with identitarian projects. The way in which the lives of labor migrants in the Gulf circle around money contributes to a reconfiguration of patriarchal power whereby individual responsibility becomes more pronounced and a calculative rationality becomes a more intuitive way to think about material and spiritual pursuits alike.

An important clue is provided by the way migration to the Gulf also influences some Christian religiosities. Ginu Zacharia Oommen (2016) has observed that Christians from the Indian state of Kerala who migrate to the Gulf often embrace neo-Pentecostal movements that reject communal Orthodox traditions, highlight individual moral responsibility, and associate the private accumulation of wealth and status with salvation. The Gulf monarchies are unlikely to have an interest in promoting evangelical Christian movements. The most important religious influence of Gulf migration should therefore be sought not in proselytization but in everyday life, in the consumerist, alienated, morally driven, forward-looking, and conservative experience of migrant life and work in the Gulf—an experience to which both Christian and Islamic revivalist movements are able to provide a compelling spiritual accompaniment.

When it becomes hegemonic, a specific religious hope or striving can become an inevitable dream, in the sense that it generates possibilities, pressures, and resources that make its pursuit compelling, even necessary as a realizable dream. But unlike building a house, we cannot empirically know in which sense and to what degree an ethical life to please God and gain his reward realizes itself. Social sciences do not possess the means to tell which consequences, if any, human action in this world may have after death. Is piety an ultimately tragic striving, or is it an eventually fruitful one? From the point of view of a search for an ethical ground for living, this is perhaps the most important question there is about God-oriented faith and piety. But ethnographic fieldwork cannot answer it. Ethnography can tell what consequences piety has in this world, and yet a key aspect of pious deeds is the hope that they will ultimately bear fruits in the afterworld.

The heuristic of two powers of imagination thus comes to its limits when dreams and strivings are primarily directed at something that is beyond the visible world. And where it does work—namely as a way to understand how some paths of hopeful action become utterly compelling while others become unlikely—it does not assign religious imagination to simply one or the other of these two powers.

In a this-worldly perspective, religious imagination appears to be an especially potent field in which some strivings for the yet-to-be-seen, some dreams of another, better world, can turn from a marginal to a powerful position. Seen this way, the turn of many Egyptian migrants and their families toward reformist, Salafi, Islamist, and other activist forms of commitment and faith does not represent simply a loss of an authentic Egyptian tradition (if one ever existed in the first place), and it is also not a case of brainwashing by a foreign ideology. Rather, it can also be seen as a cosmopolitan accomplishment of acquiring and appropriating ways of anticipating and striving for a better life, now and in the hereafter, that are motivating and fulfilling to pursue, given the kind of life that migrants lead (Stephan-Emmrich and Mirzoev 2016).

But the appropriation of revivalist religiosities was the accomplishment of an earlier generation. The Gulf's spiritual effect appeared more complex in the time of my fieldwork. At the time of my visit to Qatar in 2009, the Islamic revival was already an accomplished fact in Egypt. Unlike the older generation of Egyptian migrants who traveled to the Gulf between the 1970s and 1990s, the young men I encountered in Qatar did not appropriate reformist theology or revivalist intensity of worship during their *ghurba* (strangerhood). They already considered it normal. They had grown up with the Islamic revival, which no longer carried the power of distinction it once did—and still does in societies where Gulf migration is a recent phenomenon (Stefan-Emmrich and Mirzoev 2016).

Tawfiq's roommate Ali was among the majority of guards who prayed regularly. He was proud of it and said that it made his life orderly and gave him "mental rest" *(raha nafsiya)*. He told me:

> I prayed regularly before I came here. I have taken to it, now I have to do it. In the evening, even if I'm very tired, I have to pray first, otherwise I cannot sleep. Sometimes, even if I'm hungry and there is food ready, I have to pray first. . . . Some people start praying more regularly in the *ghurba*, while others do the opposite, and

others stay as they were before. Whichever way, it's a matter of personality.

For Egyptians of Tawfiq and Ali's generation, the spiritual outcomes of the *ghurba* (strangerhood) experience appear rather diverse. While the Gulf is an important locus of religious revivals, in Egypt today it is also an important source of cosmopolitan, upper-class liberalism (as described in the previous chapter). Different parts of the Gulf and the Arabian Peninsula are associated with different values and spiritualities. While Saudi Arabia maintains a reputation of a firmly conservative (but also highly contradictory) country that houses the two holiest sites of Islam, Dubai is often described as the city of nightlife, pleasure, and sin.

Do purity-oriented revivalist movements still offer the most compelling spiritual way to live in the world thus shaped? Generally speaking, it seems they do. For some people, however, the shape of their experience seems to give contours to other ways of imagining and acting out one's position vis-à-vis the invisible world.

In spring 2015, after more than a year of not writing and hardly reading, Tawfiq found inspiration in Islamic mysticism. Together with Bassem, his friend from the neighboring village with whom he shares an interest in poetry, he started reading Sufi classics like Jalal al-Din Rumi and Muhyiddin ibn al-'Arabi. Together, the two men attended Sufi celebrations in Cairo. When I met Tawfiq that spring, he showed me a poem recently written by his friend that he found particularly inspiring:

The Delicate Regress by the Sheikh and Comrade, Part One

> Those who have a heart, pay attention!
> People's hearts have colors, and colors have taste and energy, and the scent of the soul precedes
> Always use your souls . . .
> And do not lean on your bodies, for the senses have their detestable limits

Drink, watch, read, play, and fulfill your lives with them . . . upon you there is no fear, and you will not grieve[33]

Welcome the morning with the enthrallment it has for you . . . stand by the side of your souls while you are in love . . . turn singing into prayer, and invocation into music and drink the voices . . . don't listen.

Quench your thirst with the voice of the night and improve your relationship with things, dogs, flowers, buildings, time, your mobile phones, your beds, your libraries; your souls are the first to be adjusted, master the expanse around you without arrogance or vanity, with all singing of praise that may be . . . with the mastery of the seekers of higher love . . . wrap in the lights of your soul the weakness of your senses and ascend, move away from propositional procedures, return to your first path, examine yourselves with longing and burning love, be friends with the sun, the winds, the water, and the fire, recline on the four directions and what is above them, do not fear the sky . . . love it . . . depart toward it every moment . . . do not worship God . . . love Him passionately . . . let Him cast upon your brains his radiant light . . . do not ride horses . . . unite with their backs while you are fasting, feel their desire to race, and race . . . get drunk with the wine of flirtation and beware of getting tired . . .

Choose the words in their right place . . . Light does not suit in place of radiance, love has senses other than passion and longing, grace is not the same as beauty, the heart is one thing and the cardiac organ another, drinking does not mean quenching of thirst . . . do not stand at the doorsteps of words . . . craving foils desire

Do not give up your divine graciousness, and do not lose your balance to pretentious tension

There is no fault in the universe other than the corruption of souls

(Abu Gweily 2016, 119–22, my translation)

What drew Tawfiq, a man of long-lasting socialist convictions, to Islamic mysticism at this particular moment? He only briefly mentioned to me how this text had helped him to make sense of the contradictory reality of things. In any case, he was not alone. Since the defeated revolution of 2011, Sufism has experienced a veritable revival in Egypt.

Another friend of Tawfiq's interpreted his Sufi turn as escapism at a moment when the revolution was defeated, political freedom was non-existent, and the economic prospects for most Egyptians were miserable. Yet he too sympathized with the mystic vision of the loving God.

More often than not in the course of history, Sufism has a record of being apolitical and loyalist in relation to worldly authorities. It has often been viewed by Egyptian and Western governments as less danger-ous than Islamist movements, with their usually reformist theologies and their political drive for purity and antagonism. The current Egyptian regime actively promotes Sufism even if, at the same time, it also relies on the support of Salafi allies in Egypt and abroad. But regime support alone does not explain the newly found popularity of both traditional and eclectic Sufism (Sedgwick 2017) that I have also encountered among regime critics of Islamist and leftist leanings alike. Of the many dissent-ing visions available, Sufism is probably the least confrontational, the politically and societally most accepted, and indeed the most escapist. It comes with no political pretensions, and only seldom do its followers rally in its name for radical moral reform of society. Instead, Sufism pro-vides a space of spiritual experimentation, perhaps also a parallel space of imagining a different ordering of the world in the face of an oppres-sive reality. This seems to me the gist of Bassem's poem and a key to its inspirational power that helped Tawfiq emerge out of a period of stress and depression.

Escape is an evasive movement away from a known condition toward something unknown. Bassem's mystical sermon, with its call to a "regress" beyond the taken-for-granted structure of language and the senses, contains no action plan concerning the political economy of the hydrocarbon age. It is an expression of a search for a different way to imagine existence and, possibly, a different way to exist.

Eight years earlier, Tawfiq had phrased his plans for migration in terms of a different escape: a jump over prison walls. In the meantime, he had come to understand the nature of walls much better. Viewed from the perspective of his trajectory, Tawfiq's taking inspiration from his friend's poetic sermon of regress can be read in two contrary ways. In one reading, it is a gesture of acceptance, a way of coming to terms with a troublesome world by means of a regress toward a mystical sense of loving unity. In another reading, it tells of struggle taken to a mystical level, continuing the search for something greater and different from what the moral–financial circuit of migration commonly provides. In either case, for the time being the consequences are unknown and perhaps remain so in the world the social sciences can study.

15

THE SHINE OF THE METROPOLIS

T his is, then, what being a migrant worker in the Gulf does to one's dreams: it guides them toward a loop that reproduces and, at the same time, unsettles taken-for-granted aspirations. By channeling energies toward the dream and the work of crafting of a life that is the same but better, it reproduces societies in an altered, unsettled shape.

Villages like Nazlat al-Rayyis, with houses built and families established through migrant money, have become what may be called suburbs of the Gulf: the home of people who must travel and endure life elsewhere to make that home possible. This is not unique to Egyptian villages: it is a global condition. Suburbs of the Gulf extend not only across Egypt, but also throughout Nepal, Pakistan, India, the Philippines, and elsewhere—just as villages and towns relying on other migratory circuits exist in Eastern Europe, West Africa, Central Asia, and Central America.[34] This condition is unlikely to change as long as there persist the respective political economies of unequal wealth and income, center–periphery dependencies, and dreams that can be realized abroad.

The starting point of my fieldwork for this book was the realization that I could not understand life in Egypt without studying the effects of international migration and foreign dependency. It has subsequently become an attempt to also understand the wider world: the global processes that motivate, structure, and are structured by contemporary migrations such as Tawfiq's.

Migratory movement is nothing new in rural Egypt, contrary to the oft-repeated tourist and nationalist image of "the Egyptian village" as an ancient place rooted in the soil, unchanged for centuries or even millennia. Family names in Nazlat al-Rayyis point to a history of migrations from Upper Egypt, Syria, Palestine, Yemen, and elsewhere. Egyptian villages have been well connected to global capitalism since the nineteenth century. The modernizing Egyptian state of the nineteenth century needed villagers as labor for large construction projects and as soldiers. The system of large-scale plantations *('izab)* that dominated Egyptian agriculture from the nineteenth century until the 1960s relied on a constant flow of seasonal farm workers *(tarahil)*. Many industries in contemporary times, particularly tourism, rely on a seasonal flows of workers who come and go but do not settle (Weyland 1993; Abaza 2013). At the same time, millions of people have been moving from the countryside to the cities, a movement that had already begun in the early twentieth century. Although in many ways a continuation of earlier migratory patterns, recent migrations from Egypt to the Gulf, Europe, and North America have resulted in qualitative differences at home. International migrants can accumulate money, networks, and experience that previously were seldom available to poor people from villages. This has transformed rural Egypt (in fact, it has transformed all of Egypt: see Hoofdar 1999; Amin 2000; Ghannam 2002). It has improved living conditions in the countryside and diminished the contrast between cities and villages (Abaza 2013; Giangrande and De Bonis 2018). But migration has also created new pressures, inequalities, and conflicts. In rural and urban milieus alike it has contributed to the increasingly acute feeling of existing at the periphery of a metropolitan world that is elsewhere.

This sense that the world and its opportunities are elsewhere or "outside" *(barra* in Arabic) appears to be a widely shared sentiment across the Global South (Elliot, 2021). But similar sentiments have in the past also shaped—and continue to shape—the Global North. This is easily forgotten if we tell a history of migration only from the perspective of the metropolitan centers where migrants arrive, which brings me to a concluding comparative observation.

The Gulf states embrace the condition of global movement from provinces to metropolitan centers and exploit it systematically to their advantage. Wealthy European countries, in comparison, tend to act in more contradictory ways that generate powerful yet ultimately absurd constructs such as the migrant–refugee distinction and border regimes that are at once brutal and full of loopholes. In public discussions, curtailing the number of migrants and refugees arriving is a shared concern across the entire political spectrum (with the exception of the few proponents of open borders). Also shared is the faith that doing so is possible and feasible, be it by means of harsher border regimes (the right-wing proposal) or by improving living conditions in migrants' countries of origin (the left-wing proposal).

My native country of Finland (or, more precisely, the urban centers of southern Finland) is today one of those wealthy regions of the Global North that attracts migrants and where debates about how to deal with the arrival of new inhabitants increasingly structure political divides and societal anxieties. During my childhood in the 1970s, in contrast, Finland was a migrant-sending society. In the 1960s and 1970s, over 300,000 people (out of a population of 4.5 million) traveled as migrant workers to Sweden; approximately half of them settled permanently (Korkiasaari 2001; Heikkilä 2014). At the same time, a major migration from the countryside to cities turned Finland from a mainly rural to a mainly urban country. The population of the metropolitan area of Finland's capital Helsinki grew from approximately 350,000 in 1946 to 1.45 million in 2016 (Mäki and Vuori 2017).

The differences between Finnish and Egyptian migrations are evident. The pressing sense that one must but cannot move, so common in Egypt today, was not part of the twentieth-century Finnish experience. Egyptians today are subject to restrictive and exploitative visa and labor laws in the countries to which they travel. Finnish migrants could board the ferry to Sweden with an ID card and settle freely without having to apply for residence permits. Egyptian migrants tend to express a stronger social ideal of circular movement that is especially tangible in house-building. Finnish migrants who settled in Sweden seldom built houses in their native villages. Egyptian migrations have been driven by young men, while in Finland young women were also likely to leave. Finland shares with Sweden a long history but not the political dependency that has evolved between Egypt and the Gulf states since the 1970s. The peak of Finnish–Swedish migration was comparatively short and slowed down quickly by the 1980s as the standards of living in the two countries became more similar (Korkiasaari 2001). In Egypt, pressure to migrate continues forty years after the onset of mass labor migration, and the income gap between Egypt and the Gulf states has actually increased, becoming far more extreme than it ever was between Sweden and Finland (Alvaredo et al. 2018).[35]

And yet the parallels are intriguing. The first parallel casts doubt on the right-wing proposal of strengthening borders. In the presence and absence of border controls and visa regimes alike, some people move and some stay. Nobody prevented my parents' generation from moving to Sweden. My mother's best friend left for Sweden; my mother did not. Enormous international border regimes have been installed to keep people from Africa and the Middle East from moving to Western Europe (Dzenovska 2014; Gaibazzi et al. 2017): in the absence of such regimes, more people from these regions would probably come. But even with those regimes in place, people keep departing in great numbers as long as they can reasonably hope to earn more money and obtain better living conditions. The human cost of restrictive migratory regimes is terrible. In Europe, it results in deaths during dangerous crossings and years of life wasted in limbo while waiting for a crossing and then for a legal status. Paradoxically, Europe's border regime has not made migration to Europe less attractive, but it has made return more difficult for recent migrants (Elliot, 2021).

The second parallel complicates the left-wing proposal, of improving the conditions of would-be migrants' home countries. Rural Finland after World War II and rural Egypt at the turn of the twentieth and twenty-first centuries both experienced rapid population growth, an improvement of material conditions, an increase in rural poor people's expectations of living conditions, the insufficiency of traditional livelihoods to fulfill those expectations, and increased mobility and access to education and urban careers. What attracts people from villages to cities worldwide is not simply poverty but the prospect of material and existential well-being. The dream of migration appears to be at its most urgent when living conditions have already started to improve.

This is something I have witnessed during my two decades of fieldwork in Egypt. People I know in rural areas possess more things and enjoy more comfortable housing conditions. Compared to the generations of their parents and grandparents, they are more likely to have higher education degrees and they work more often in technical, commercial, and white-collar professions rather than in agriculture or fishing. But they do not feel better. On the contrary, they complain of pressure, are often stressed and exhausted, and many are in debt. A moderate improvement in material conditions has come at the cost of a sharp increase in needs, expectations, and pressures. These pressures are further aggravated by the combination of economic policies that promote competition over solidarity and a violently repressive political regime that rigs the competition in favor of those connected with the deep state. This is the condition that makes the hope of migration "forceful," as Alice Elliot (2016) has described it. Moderate improvements of living conditions do not diminish the forcefulness of that hope. Only near parity can do so—which is what has happened between Finland and Sweden since the 1980s. And even then, the movement from rural areas to urban centers continues.

Compared to Tawfiq, his family, friends and colleagues, my trajectory of movement is privileged in terms of citizenship, ethnicity, mobility, income, access to free education and public study scholarships. I could afford to make what my Egyptian friend in Sweden called bohemian decisions, such as that of becoming an anthropologist. But we share a world in which provincial locations no longer exist for themselves and instead exist in the shadow, or rather: the shine of metropolitan centers and the attraction they exert as places of opportunity. Just as Nazlat al-Rayyis and other villages worldwide are suburbs of the Gulf, so also cities, even entire countries, exist in a suburban position toward national, regional, and global metropolitan centers. In that same world, metropolitan centers inevitably become more diverse. This is a process that unsettles all rooted, localized forms of living—sometimes openly, and sometimes in ways that are not acknowledged. Its unsettling capacity makes this process a fertile breeding ground for exclusionist, identitarian movements and cosmopolitan explorations alike. In the world that emerges, the problem is not how to change things; change is abundant and accelerates (Eriksen 2016). The more daunting and fantastic task is how to live a conservative life where one can trust that things and people remain in their anticipated places.

Final Chapter

ECONOMY IS NOT RATIONAL,

AND FANTASY IS NOT FREE

The online Arabic dictionary *Almaany* gives the following meanings for the word *hulm*, which in Egypt is pronounced *hilm*:

- What the sleeper sees in his sleep. . . .
- What appears far from reality: *'Every young man hopes to realize his dreams.'*[36]

The dictionary also gives a number of idiomatic expressions that elaborate the second sense of *hulm/hilm* as idealized or unreal hope, such as *sleeper's dreams (ahlam na'im)* explained as "false hopes," and *the boy of dreams (fata al-ahlam)* explained as "the imaginary shape *(sura khayaliya)* of a young man in the consciousness of a girl who wishes him as her husband." The specialist terminology of dream interpretation in Arabic furthermore distinguishes between *hulm/hilm* as a dream that comes from the sleeper's subconscious or from Satan and *ru'ya* as a true dream vision from God (Mittermaier 2011). In its sleeping and waking varieties alike, Arabic *hulm/hilm* thus brings together *non-reality* and *desire*.

Dreams are a form of imagination, but not all imagination is unreal. The Arabic word for imagination, *khayal*, also means shadow, reflection in mirror or water, dream image, shadow play, and scarecrow. Etymologically, *khayal* is not a faculty of the mind but an *immaterial shape*. In a similar manner, the English *imagination* is derived from the Latin *imago*, the meanings of which include image, likeness, ghost, and echo. In Sufi Muslim traditions, *khayal* is a way to access the unseen realm, which in the mystical understanding is a higher order of reality (Mittermaier 2011). In contemporary social sciences, imagination emerges as an intangible but highly consequential way to structure shared realities—such as in "imagined communities" (Anderson 1991), "the imaginary institution of society" (Castoriadis 1987), and "the imagination itself as a social practice" (Appadurai 1996).

Dreams of the waking kind, in contrast, thrive on *the desire to make something unreal real*. The young Egyptian migrant workers with whom I spoke insisted that only by having and pursuing a dream could they endure their predicaments. A dream, in the sense about which they spoke, is a site of potentiality, located primarily in the future. However, it makes a difference whether a dream is recognized as an unlikely fantasy or is taken to be something that is not yet realized but can and should be, the sooner the better.

This ambiguity of dream/*hilm* between something worth striving for and something hopelessly unrealistic is a good entry point to thinking about migration as an instance of imagination as a social practice. Since the 1990s, anthropological theories of imagination and the imaginary have become part of the common stock of the trade (Strauss 2006), allowing us to look at the assumed, the expected, and the fantastic in different ways, ranging from the constitution of societies and currencies (money and nation-states being prime examples of extremely powerful realities that are essentially imaginary; see Ho 2005; Anderson 1991) to the way media, fiction, and simulation provide us compelling models—some promising, others terrifying—for our intimate lives and political engagements alike (Starrett 2009; Masquelier 2009; Schielke 2016). This proliferation of often quite divergent approaches taken under the title of imagination or the imaginary has compelled me to specify my focus, as follows.

While inspired by Abdelmalek Sayad's (1999) work on migrant workers' illusions and disappointments, in this book I have argued that migrants' initial aspirational dreams are not simply disappointed but rather transformed by experience. While more or less in agreement with Cornelius Castoriadis (1987) about there being an "imaginary institution of society," I have looked more specifically toward the dynamic and productive work of aspirational dreams. While drawing on Appadurai's intervention, I have argued that imagination as a social practice can perform different sorts of work. In critical recognition of the widespread neoliberal discourse promoting fantasy, innovation, and inventiveness—pronounced in the way Arab Gulf societies represent themselves—I have pointed out that rather than being freely available, dreams are a scarce resource.

With the focus on dreams, I am also more widely concerned with the sorts of imagining that are openly acknowledged as such: literary and cinematic fiction, nighttime dreams, fantasies, utopias, and aspirational dreams. Quite unlike with money and the nation, these are forms of imagination whereby acknowledging their current non-reality is essential to entertaining them. These imaginings relate in different ways to questions about their possible realization, which gives them different sorts of material power. In the course of this book, I have elaborated what in my view are two powers associated with aspirational dreams—one confirming, directing, and narrowing down the scope of action, and another questioning, confusing, and widening it. Labor migration is one of those experiences where the tension between these two powers is sharply felt.

A risk involved in this approach is that it may slip into a romantic search for "agency" in the face of "structure," whereby the weaker, other dreams would be taken to be the authentic, "agentic" ones. The lure of a romantic approach is great; indeed, some people have described their experiences to me in such terms. They have told me of instances where others have dismissed their dreams or hindered them from pursuing them. I have often encountered "society" *(al-mugtama')* being referred to in that capacity, as the collective entity that foils individual dreams.

And yet social scientists and historians have repeatedly argued that the capacity to desire and to strive is grounded in and made possible by specific cultural, social, economic, and ecological configurations. Karl Marx (1961, 9–10) diagnosed a determining force of the relations of production. Pierre Bourdieu (1984) grounded the capacity of aesthetic judgment and aspiration in embodied habitus and social fields. Michel Foucault (1977; 1984) analyzed the discursive formations that constitute specific ways of being human. Currently influential proposals within anthropology include Eduardo Vivieiros de Castro's (2003) plea to recognize and to valorize the different ontologies of peoples, as well as Saba Mahmood's (2005) argument that agentic action takes place within rather than against traditions that structure our will and imagination. On a more urgent note, Alf Hornborg (2011) has argued that an unlimited potential of human growth and technological solutions is a "cultural illusion" based on concealing the dependency of our economy on the destruction of ecological resources.

In comparison to these different analyses, the vision of the self-determining, autonomous individual promoted in liberal political theory appears thin and out of touch with reality. Humans are probably never autonomous and self-determined (and when they seem to be, it is thanks to invisible forms of support, infrastructure, privilege, and resource exploitation). However, what humans make of that which forms them—the relations of production, ecologies, habitus, discourses, cultures, ontologies, or traditions that shape individual morality and will—is not deterministic, at least not in a way that contemporary social science is capable of perceiving. Otherwise, there would be no other dreams, and nobody would complain about their absence. Rather than being either deterministic or self-determined, human trajectories generally demonstrate that there is a certain range of ways to assemble and combine the knowledge, skills, and techniques one has learned. This is the stuff from which our lives are made, and yet seldom does it reproduce that which is promised in a straightforward fashion.

Rather, human lives bring together different experiences and strivings, different (and sometimes even quite opposed) ways of being moral, various moral and amoral pursuits, experiences of success and failure, relations of power, and unpredictable circumstances and consequences. Some of them may go against the grain of a societal ethos: in such situations, individual dreams seem hindered by society's lack of imagination. Otherwise, individual dreams are also shared dreams, and the conflicts that emerge are less between the individual and the collective and more between strivings and outcomes, as well as between different, competing strivings. It is in this framework of possible and actual consequences, rather than in the futile debate regarding structure versus agency, that the question about different kinds of dreams poses itself.

This existential mode of inquiry, as it may be called, has also recently gained more prominence in studies of migration conducted in the social sciences. The study of migration has been long dominated by a focus on financial flows, economic effects, and the social impact upon "receiving societies" (for important early exceptions, see Sayad 1999; Schiffauer 1991). More recently, the study of migrations and diasporas has witnessed an increasing shift toward the imaginative, the experiential, and the spiritual, along with a shift toward translocal (Freitag and von Oppen 2010) or transnational (Glick Schiller and Çağlar 2010) attempts to consider together the different sites affected by migrations.

My research has followed in the footsteps of these shifts, and it is aligned with an emerging line of research on migration and movement from an existential perspective,[37] focusing on the motivations, experiences, and subjective and intersubjective engagements in a world where migration has become such a powerful source of this worldly optimism that it has been transformed into something like a force of necessity (Alpes 2012; Elliot 2016).

However, we should not mistake the financial, legal, and political as distinct from or opposed to the existential, imaginative, and aspirational. Migrants have often told me about migration as an existential pursuit in which money plays a central role. How can we give a truthful account of the imaginative, moral, and calculative aspects of the migratory experience without reducing one aspect to another?

The Gulf migratory circuit is a privileged site to pursue such questions. Current research on migration to the Gulf has given remarkable attention to the lives, paths, and networks of migrants to and in the Gulf states, the exploitation of migrant labor in the political economy of oil states, the role of migrants in Gulf cities and societies, and the making and remaking of livelihoods in the places from which migrant workers hail.[38] Researchers working on the Gulf have also developed important lines of inquiry about diasporic lives and informal citizenship, in contrast to reducing migrants to their role as a labor force (see, for example, Vora 2013; Kanna 2010). However, I think that at least with the majority of low-income workers (and this book tells about them), labor remains a key category. But rather than thinking of migrants as an undifferentiated and exploited labor pool, I have tried to provide an account of the subjective experience of being part of the Gulf's migrant labor force.

I have also tried to consider the Gulf and Egypt together, as parts of the same circuit of movement and power regimes. To look at a site where migrants arrive without looking at the places from where migrants hail (and to where they may eventually return) is to look at only one half of the migratory process. This is, of course, the case with all migrations, but it is more evident in the Gulf than elsewhere, because the labor regime of the Gulf states imposes a circular, temporary logic on migration (Hanieh 2011).

In the course of this book, I have worked toward a non-dichotomous account about acting in a world that is not of one's own making—one in which structure and agency, individuals and collectives, moral and economic pursuits do not appear as opposites but instead come together in a meaningful account of what it means to live a life. Looking at migration from the point of view of dreams, we see the world as a place where the economy is not rational and fantasy is not free.

Rationality—in the sense popularized by neoclassical economics—is about interest-based choice of means in the face of scarcity. Freedom—in the popular, romantic sense—is about the ability to choose from an abundant multitude of possibilities, ideas, and paths of action. Common sense seems to link rationality with economy and economy with scarcity, and freedom with fantasy and fantasy with abundance. Upon closer examination, however, economy and fantasy each appear to involve both scarcity and abundance. Indeed, they may not even be different processes. A surplus of desire and anticipation exceeding the here-and-now appears to be a fundamental driving force in human societies. But there is a scarcity of conceivable ways of structuring and channeling that excess. Money-making, house-building, and imperial power all involve considerations about and the accumulation of limited available means toward specific ends. And yet in addition to the question about how to act in the face of scarcity, economic paths of action always also involve considerations about how to spend the surplus.[39]

There are niches within the global capitalist process where exploitation of other people's scarcity (such as the need for carbon-based energy or migrant workers' need for money to build a life and maintain a family) provides some people such material abundance that imagination can appear to be the only limit. Imagination is indeed the limit, but in a more complex and fundamental way than advertising boards in the Gulf would have us believe.

Writing about real estate projects and urbanism in the Gulf states, Christian Steiner argues that their hyperreal extravagance is a strategy to turn oil wealth into symbolic capital, a way to generate dominance through awe-inspiring, superlative megaprojects: "[T]he more hyperreal and iconic urban spaces become, the more they contribute to the legitimization and stabilization of given structures of power and rule" (Steiner 2014, 28). I wonder, however, how strategic this strategy really is. Just as the moral logic of building a life structures the Egyptian worker's struggle to earn money, the Gulf states' drive to create superlative spectacles may be rooted in moral and ideological imperatives that structure the Gulf elites' striving for dominance and in their imaginings about how their surplus earnings might be spent. Perhaps such grandeur simply indicates the limits of the Gulf elites' capacity to dream. In any event, the cut-and-paste hyperreal fantasy world of the Gulf is indeed a system of domination capable of creating inescapable realities worldwide. It is a feature of the first power of imagination, the capacity of dreams to reproduce and reinforce relations of power.

Such processes are material as well as imagined—imagined not only in the sense of being unreal yet desired but also in the sense that material resources and obstacles are inseparable from the anticipation of what is and what is not possible and desirable. From the point of view of a critical social science, one tasked not only with describing how humans live together but also with providing critique and alternative visions, this means that the search for radical potentials toward a different world may require some rethinking. To strive for normality may be as world-changing (or also as world-maintaining) as the struggle for radical change. What is radical often has less potential to be realized, with the opposite also often being the case: realization tends to turn radical strivings into normal ones, accompanied by the ordinary, undramatic power and value of conformity that is part of every striving for a normal life. Alternative dreams are possible and may even become powerful, but only if they are able to generate the self-reinforcing dynamic of imagination and production that results in material outcomes that make it compelling and likely to struggle for the sake of such dreams.

NOTES

1 Not his real name. For the sake of privacy, I do not mention people, companies, or work sites by their actual names. Similarly, Tawfiq's home village of Nazlat al-Rayyis only goes by that name in my writing.

2 Smart Village Egypt is an actual prestige project of the Mubarak regime established in 2003 and inspired by similar projects in the Gulf; see Elsheshtawy 2013, 112–13.

3 Counting children and grandchildren born of two brothers married to two sisters but excluding spouses and in-laws.

4 This is not true of all migrant groups, though. For example, well-off people from India have created diasporic communities with generational continuity in the United Arab Emirates (Vora 2013). Among Egyptians with high income levels, there is a characteristic pattern of parents returning by retirement age at the latest and of children returning, as it were, to Egypt for their university education after going to school in the Gulf.

5 The following is inspired by discussions I have had in Egypt in 2016 and 2017 with readers and audiences of the Arabic version of this book.

6 Such "cultivation of impermanence" (Mbodj-Pouye 2016) is not unique to migration to the Gulf. In Europe, it is common among first generations of migrants, but it tends to become more complicated the longer people stay, and especially if their children stay or migrate as well.

7 Other anthropologists who have done more long-term research among workers in the Gulf have the advantage of a substantial understanding of the different facets of society and positions in the labor system inhabited by migrant workers—an understanding that I cannot claim. But the difficulty in accessing work sites and housing sometimes compels researchers to content themselves with what

Caroline Osella (Andrew Gardner 2012a, 25) has called "Friday ethnography," based on meeting workers only on their day off.

8   Security workers occupy a paradoxical position in the labor regime. They are subjected to the same system of exploitation, but they are also part of the regime that maintains the system of privilege, inequality, and authoritarian rule. The people with whom I stayed in Qatar were not involved in these tasks, but many migrant workers do, in fact, make their living by policing other migrants. In Gulf countries that have faced large-scale protest movements, such as Bahrain and Saudi Arabia, the security force suppressing these home-grown protest movements was also largely made up of migrant workers (see Davidson 2014; Hanieh 2011).

9   Bahrain, Kuwait, Dubai, and Qatar have in recent years made some exceptions to the system, such as allowing the government rather than individuals to act directly as the *kafil* (sponsor) or banning employers from withholding workers' passports. They also now allow some direct foreign investment (one feature of the *kafala* regime is that foreign investors must have a citizen–partner who owns 51% of the joint venture), but none of the Gulf states seem interested in fully abolishing the *kafala* system (see Davidson 2014; Mednicoff 2012).

10   For figures regarding the salaries and savings of low-income workers in Qatar, see Andrew Gardner 2011, 9.

11   During the first week and a half of my fieldwork in Doha, I stayed in a hotel and then accepted Tawfiq and his roommates' invitation to share their room.

12   Among the Egyptians, a laptop was often the first thing purchased with their savings. In 2009, smartphones had just entered the market and were still too expensive for migrant workers. The workers would usually also buy a new phone as soon as they could, but for communicating online, a laptop was still indispensable in 2009.

13   Statistics about the countries of origin of migrant workers in Qatar are not public, and I have not been able to confirm from other sources the claim that a quota exists to maintain a Muslim majority.

14   In the years that followed, there were much larger strikes across the Gulf countries in the wake of the global financial crisis. But even those strikes, though much larger, did not see the emergence of a shared class consciousness among migrant workers (see Hanieh 2011, 191–92).

15   This does not mean that they would not be annoyed and troubled in other contexts. An Egyptian woman who had worked in the medical field in Saudi Arabia told me that she faced near constant sexual harassment by her male colleagues and superiors at her workplace.

16 When used in the context of romantic and sexual relations, the word "cultivated" *(muthaqqaf)* has a clear erotic intention in Egyptian Arabic, meaning the mastery of flirtation and sexual gamesmanship. Following the same logic, the colloquial euphemism for a porn film is "cultural film" *(film thaqafi)*.

17 See, for example, Sayad 1999; Alpes 2012; Andrew Gardner 2012b; Swarowsky and Schielke 2009; Swarowsky 2014; Pelican 2014.

18 This is not always the case. I know one mother in the village who keeps herself informed about the minute details of her sons' lives and hardships in Saudi Arabia.

19 The way in which some people back home cultivate a kind of optimistic ignorance about working conditions abroad (while they may be very knowledgeable about other issues) has been described in strikingly similar shapes by anthropologists working in different locations, such as Algeria (Sayad 1999); Cameroon (Alpes 2012); and Morocco (Elliot, 2021).

20 My thinking is inspired here by Pierre Bourdieu's (1984) thinking of habitus as a way to strive for one's given position in a social hierarchy, although Bourdieu does not speak about dreams, and by Michael Jackson's (2011) idea of the search for a good life "within limits," although Jackson does not speak of it as inevitable.

21 The ideal and often practiced model of housing in rural areas and also informal urban areas is a house where each son has a floor of his own for his wife and children.

22 I relate this argument to existing research on imagination in more detail in the last chapter.

23 In her research with women in a Moroccan rural region who have married migrants to Europe, Alice Elliot (2021) has noted that even when their status and means are otherwise limited, migrant men enjoy a major advantage on the marriage market because they embody "the outside" on which a migratory society depends and thrives. In Egypt as well, migrant men are surrounded by an aura of possibility and opportunity that cannot be reduced to their financial means.

24 In the conventional family ideal in Egypt, the husband should be the sole breadwinner and the wife's income is for her private use. The reality of Egyptian families is often different, and women commonly contribute a large part or even the majority of the family's income. That reality does not diminish the power of the conventional ideal— rather, it puts additional pressure upon men should they not be able to provide for their families, while women's contributions are rendered invisible.

25 To appease the population, various Egyptian governments raised
    public sector salaries several times between 2011 and 2013. In 2013,
    salaries rose higher than the rate of inflation (*Mada Masr* 2013). But
    by autumn 2014, that increase had already been reversed by high
    inflation.

26 Davidson (2014) argues that this was motivated by an attempt by the
    Gulf monarchies to prevent political unrest among their citizens by
    offering them even more jobs.

27 According to the very optimistic official estimate, revenue would
    increase from $5.3 billion in 2014 to over $13 billion in 2023. In the
    following years, revenue actually declined and only began to rise by
    2017, reaching a record $5.6 billion in the fiscal year 2017–18 (CEIC
    Data 2019; Esterman 2015; Reuters 2015; 2018).

28 According to World Bank data, remittance inflow was 11.8 percent
    of Egypt's GDP in 2018 (https://www.knomad.org/sites/default/
    files/2019-04/Remittance%20Inflows%20Apr%202019.xlsx).

29 In a manner echoing François Bayart's (2000) thesis about
    extraversion—that is, the reliance on foreign dependency as a source
    of power and income—Egyptian foreign and financial policy has for
    a long time relied on shifting relations of dependency toward the
    United States, the Soviet Union/Russia, Western Europe, and the Gulf
    monarchies. In the past two or three decades, the influence of Gulf
    monarchies has increased. The revolutionary period since 2011 did
    not interrupt this dependency, but it did result in a shift in alliances:
    The short-lived government of the Muslim Brotherhood after the
    revolution in 2011 relied on support from Qatar. The new regime that
    came to power in 2013 relies on support from Saudi Arabia and the
    United Arab Emirates, and Egypt's relations with Qatar have since
    become strained.

30 For Egypt, see Elsheshtawy 2013; Adham 2014. For comparative cases,
    see Pelican 2014 on West Africa; Stephan-Emmrich and Mirzoev 2016
    on Central Asia.

31 See, for example, Dalakoglou 2010 on Albania; Mbodj-Pouye and
    Michalon 2013 on Mali; Bürkle and Erdem 2016 on Turkey.

32 Sometimes, this topos is paired with a parallel one arguing that
    migration of conservative rural people to cities turned Egypt from
    a modern, civilized country into a backward, rural conglomerate.
    Indeed, some quantitative evidence suggests that rural–urban migrants
    are more likely to support Islamic political movements than people
    with long-standing urban roots (this was clearly reflected in the results
    of the 2011 and 2012 elections; see Ali 2012; Schewe 2012). However,
    the claim that Egypt was a less rural-conservative country before

the 1960s is obviously a stereotype insofar that it equates "Egypt" with a small demographic of urban residents from before the mass urbanization that began in the 1970s.

33 This is an intertextual reference to a verse of the Qur'an on "friends of God" *(awliya' Allah)*, who in the Sufi tradition are understood to mean those who have a special, close relationship with God similar to sainthood: *Indeed upon the friends of God there is no fear, nor do they grieve* (Qur'an 10:62, my translation).

34 See, for example, Bouzas 2018; Elliot, 2021; Katy Gardner 1995; Osella and Osella 2007; Reeves 2015; Weyland 1993.

35 Sweden's gross national income per capita was 50 percent higher than Finland's in 1970. Qatar's gross national income per capita in 2017 was more than twenty times higher than Egypt's. For a comparison of Egypt and selected Gulf states, see https://data.worldbank.org/indicator/NY.GNP.PCAP.KD?locations=SA-EG-AE-QA; for Finland and Sweden, see https://data.worldbank.org/indicator/NY.GNP.PCAP.KD?locations=FI-SE.

36 https://www.almaany.com/ar/dict/ar ar/%D8%AD%D9%84%D9%85/

37 See, for example, Hage 2005; Lucht 2011; Graw and Schielke 2012; Jackson 2013; Jackson and Piette 2015; Gaibazzi 2015b; Elliot 2015; Reeves 2015; Lems 2016; Tošić and Palmberger 2016; and Lems and Tošić 2019.

38 See, for example, Ghannam 2002; Osella and Osella 2007; Gruntz 2012b; Davidson 2014;   2010; Andrew Gardner 2010; 2012a; 2012b; Kamrava and Babar 2012; Gruntz and Pagès El-Karoui 2013; Kanna 2013; Hanieh 2011; Pelican 2014; Wippel et al. 2014; Fernandez and de Regt 2014; Jain and Oommen 2016; Stephan-Emmrich and Mirzoev 2016; Bouzas 2018.

39 This thought is inspired by Michael Jackson's (2011, xii) argument about the anticipation of more than exists in the here and now being a fundamental human capacity, as well as by Georges Bataille's (1991) hyperbolic but instructive claim that expenditure of surplus rather than scarcity is the key problem of political economy.

BIBLIOGRAPHY

Abaza, Mona. 2013. *The Cotton Plantation Remembered: An Egyptian Family Story*. Cairo: American University in Cairo Press.

Abenante, Paola. 2015. "The Ambiguity of Virtue: Expectations and Experiences of Piety in the Life of a Young Egyptian Woman." *Ricerca Folklorica* 69: 39–53.

Abu Gweily, Bassem Muhammed. 2016. *Ka-bidayat aniqa li-'itr untha: shi'r fusha*. Cairo: Egyptian General Book Organization.

Adham, Khaled. 2014. "Modes of Urban Diffusion: Culture, Politics and the Impact of the Recent Urban Developments in the Arabian Gulf Cities." In *Under Construction: Logics of Urbanism in the Gulf Region*, edited by Steffen Wippel, Katrin Bromber, Christian Steiner, and Birgit Krawietz, 233–45. Surrey: Ashgate.

Ali, Amro. 2012. "Sons of Beaches: How Alexandria's Ideological Battles Shape Egypt." *Jadaliyya*, December 29, 2012. http://www.jadaliyya.com/Details/27724/Sons-of-Beaches-How-Alexandria%60s-Ideological-Battles-Shape-Egypt.

Alpes, Maybritt Jill. 2012. "Bushfalling: The Making of Migratory Expectations in Anglophone Cameroon." In *The Global Horizon: Expectations of Migration in Africa and the Middle East*, edited by Knut Graw and Samuli Schielke, 43–58. Leuven: Leuven University Press.

Alvaredo, Facundo, Lydia Assouad, and Thomas Piketty. 2018. "Measuring Inequality in the Middle East 1990–2016: The World's Most Unequal Region?" *WID.world Working Paper Series 2017/15*. https://wid.world/document/alvaredoassouadpiketty-middleeast-widworldwp201715/.

Amin, Galal. 2000. *Whatever Happened to the Egyptians? Changes in Egyptian Society from 1950 to the Present*. Cairo: American University in Cairo Press.

Anderson, Benedict. 1991. *Imagined Communities: Reflections on the Origin and Spread of Nationalism*. London and New York: Verso.

Appadurai, Arjun. 1996. *Modernity at Large: Cultural Dimensions of Globalization*. Minneapolis: University of Minnesota Press.

———. 2013. *The Future as Cultural Fact: Essays on the Global Condition*. London: Verso.

el-Aswad, El-Sayed. 2004. "Viewing the World through Upper Egyptian Eyes: From Regional Crisis to Global Blessing." In *Upper Egypt: Identity and Change*, edited by Nicholas Hopkins and Reem Saad, 55–78. Cairo: American University in Cairo Press.

Bataille, Georges. 1991 [1949]. *The Accursed Share: Vol. 1, Consumption*. Translated by Robert Hurley. New York: Zone Books.

Baudrillard, Jean. 1993. *Symbolic Exchange and Death*. London: Sage.

Bayart, Jean-François. 2000. "Africa in the World: A History of Extraversion." *African Affairs* 99: 217–67.

Bourdieu, Pierre. 1984. *Distinction: A Social Critique of the Judgement of Taste*. London: Routledge.

Bouzas, Antía Mato. 2018. "From the Karakoram Mountains to the Gulf: Migration, Development and Religion in the Making of Transnational Spaces." *ZMO Working Papers* 21. http://d-nb.info/1176721798/34.

Bürkle, Stefanie, and Fulya Erdem. 2016. "Ein Dorf voller Villen, ohne Bewohner / A Village Full of Villas But without People." In *Migration von Räumen / Migrating Spaces: Architektur und Identität im Kontext türkischer Remigration / Architecture and Identity in the Context of Turkish Remigration*, edited by Stefanie Bürkle, 237–34. Berlin: Vice Versa Verlag.

Business & Human Rights Resource Centre. 2018. "Qatar Announces Significant Labour Reforms for Migrant Workers, Technical Cooperation Agreement with ILO; Rights Groups Call for Follow-Through on Implementation." https://www.business-humanrights.org/en/qatariilo-agreement-on-labour-reforms-must-be-backed-by-action-real-improvements-for-migrant-workers-say-rights-groups.

Cantini, Daniele, and Lucile Gruntz. 2010. "Des nouveaux riches aux jeunes martyrs: les évolutions de la migration de travail égyptienne au prisme de ses représentations médiatiques." In *Chroniques égyptiennes 2008*, edited by Iman Farag, 79–118. Cairo: CEDEJ.

Castoriadis, Cornelius. 1987. *The Imaginary Institution of Society*. Translated by Kathleen Blamey. Cambridge, MA: MIT Press.

CEIC Data. 2019. "Egypt Maritime Transport: Suez Canal Revenues: Annual Ending June." https://www.ceicdata.com/en/egypt/

maritime-transport-revenues maritime-transport-suez-canal
-revenues-annual-ending-june.

Coelho, Paolo. 1996. *Al-Khaymiya'i* [The Alchemist]. Translated by Bahaa
Taher. Cairo: Dar al-Hilal.

Dalakoglou, Dimitri. 2010. "Migrating-remitting-'building'-dwelling:
House-making as 'Proxy' Presence in Postsocialist Albania." *Journal of
the Royal Anthropological Institute* 16 (4): 761–77.

Davidson, Christopher M. 2014. "Expatriates and the Gulf Monarchies:
Politics, Security and the Arab Spring." *Asian Affairs* 45 (2): 270–88.

Debord, Guy. 1977 [1967]. *The Society of the Spectacle*. Translated by Fredy
Perlman. Detroit: Black & Red.

De Certeau, Michel. 1984. *The Practice of Everyday Life*. Translated by Steven
Rendall. Berkeley: University of California Press.

De Genova, Nicholas P. 2002. "Migrant 'Illegality' and Deportability in
Everyday Life." *Annual Review of Anthropology* 31: 419–47.

Dunqul, Amal. 2005 [1962]. "Kalimat Spartacus al-akhira." In *Al-a'mal
al-kamila*, 91–97. Cairo: Maktabat Madbuli.

Dzenovska, Dace. 2014. "Bordering Encounters, Sociality and Distribution
of the Ability to Live a 'Normal Life.'" *Social Anthropology/Anthropologie
Sociale* 22 (3): 271–87.

Elliot, Alice. 2015. "Paused Subjects: Waiting for Migration in North
Africa." *Time & Society* 25 (1): 102–16.

———. 2016. "Forceful Hope." *Allegra Lab*, April 26, 2016. http://
allegralaboratory.net/forceful-hope/.

———. 2021. *The Outside: Migration and the Imagination of Life in Morocco*.
Bloomington: Indiana University Press.

Elliot, Alice, and Laura Menin. 2018. "For an Anthropology of Destiny."
HAU: Journal of Ethnographic Theory 8 (1/2): 292–99.

Elsheshtawy, Yasser. 2010. *Dubai: Behind an Urban Spectacle*. London:
Routledge.

———. 2013. "Resituating the Dubai Spectacle." In *The Superlative City:
Dubai and the Urban Condition in the Early Twenty-First Century*, edited
by Ahmed Kanna, 105–21. Cambridge, MA; Harvard University Graduate School of Design.

Eriksen, Thomas Hylland. 2016. *Overheating: An Anthropology of Accelerated
Change*. London: Pluto Press.

Esterman, Isabel. 2015. "A Reality Check on the New Suez Canal." *Mada
Masr*, August 3, 2015. http://www.madamasr.com/sections/economy/
reality-check-new-suez-canal.

Fernandez, Bina, and Marina de Regt, eds. 2014. *Migrant Domestic Workers in the Middle East: The Home and the World*. London: Palgrave MacMillan.

Fortier, Corinne, Aymon Kreil, and Irene Maffi, eds. 2016. "Love in the Arab World." Special section in *Arab Studies Journal* 24 (2): 96–175.

Foucault, Michel. 1977. *Discipline and Punish: The Birth of Prison*. New York: Pantheon Books.

———. 1984. *L'usage des plaisirs*. Vol. 2 of *Histoire de la sexualité*. Paris: Gallimard.

———. 2007. *Security, Territory, Population: Lectures at the Collège de France 1977–1978*. Edited by Michel Senellart. Translated by Graham Burchell. London: Palgrave Macmillan.

Freitag, Ulrike, and Achim von Oppen, eds. 2010. *Translocality: The Study of Globalising Processes from a Southern Perspective*. Leiden: Brill.

Gaibazzi, Paolo. 2015a. *Bush Bound: Young Men and Rural Permanence in Migrant West Africa*. New York: Berghahn.

———. 2015b. "The Quest for Luck: Fate, Fortune, Work and the Unexpected among Gambian Soninke Hustlers." *Critical African Studies* 7 (3): 227–42.

Gaibazzi, Paolo, Alice Bellagamba, and Stephan Dünnwald, eds. 2017. *EurAfrican Borders and Migration Management: Political Cultures, Contested Spaces, and Ordinary Lives*. London: Palgrave Macmillan.

Gardner, Andrew. 2010. *City of Strangers: Gulf Migration and the Indian Community in Bahrain*. Ithaca, NY: Cornell University Press

———. 2011. "Gulf Migration and the Family." *Journal of Arabian Studies* 1: 3–25.

———. 2012a. "Rumour and Myth in the Labour Camps of Qatar." *Anthropology Today* 28, no. 6: 25–28.

———. 2012b. "Why Do They Keep Coming? Labor Migrants in the Gulf States." In *Migrant Labor in the Persian Gulf*, edited by Mehran Kamrava and Zahra Babar, 41–58. London: Hurst; New York: Columbia University Press.

Gardner, Katy. 1995. *Global Migrants, Local Lives: Travel and Transformation in Rural Bangladesh*. Oxford: Clarendon Press.

Ghannam, Farha. 2002. *Remaking the Modern: Space, Relocation, and the Politics of Identity*. Berkeley: University of California Press.

———. 2013. *Live and Die Like a Man: Gender Dynamics in Urban Egypt*. Stanford, CA: Stanford University Press.

Giangrande, Francesca, and Luciano De Bonis. 2018. "Identity in Transformation of Rural Egyptian Villages." In *Cities' Identity Through*

Architecture and Arts, edited by Anna Catalani et al., 517–24. London: Taylor & Francis.

Glick Schiller, Nina, and Ayşe Çağlar, eds. 2010. *Locating Migration: Rescaling Cities and Migrants*. Ithaca: Cornell University Press.

Gräf, Bettina, and Jakob Skovgaard-Petersen, eds. 2009. *The Global Mufti: The Phenomenon of Yusuf al-Qaradawi*. London: Hurst.

Graw, Knut. 2012. "On the Cause of Migration: Being and Nothingness in the African-European Border Zone." In *The Global Horizon: Expectations of Migration in Africa and the Middle East*, edited by Knut Graw and Samuli Schielke, 23–42. Leuven: Leuven University Press.

Graw, Knut, and Samuli Schielke, eds. 2012. *The Global Horizon: Expectations of Migration in Africa and the Middle East*. Leuven: Leuven University Press.

Gruntz, Lucile. 2012a. "Le Retour des citoyens: émigration de retour du Golfe et évolutions sociales au Caire (1971–2011)." PhD thesis, EHESS, Paris.

———. 2012b. "La 'révolution' du Golfe au Caire? Émigration de travail vers les monarchies pétrolières et changements sociopolitiques en Égypte." *Migrations Société* 24 (143): 1–14.

Gruntz, Lucile, and Delphine Pagès El-Karoui. 2013. "Migration and Family Change in Egypt: A Comparative Approach to Social Remittances." *Migration Letters* 10 (1): 71–79.

Hage, Ghassan. 2005. "A Not So Multi-Sited Ethnography of a Not So Imagined Community." *Anthropological Theory* 5 (4): 463–75.

al-Haj Saleh, Yassin. 2017. "Freedom: Home, Prison, Exile . . . and the World." Translated by Rana Issa. Yassin al-Haj Saleh, April 3, 2017. http://www.yassinhs.com/2017/04/03/yassin-al-haj-saleh-on-freedom-home-prison-exileand-the-world/.

Hanieh, Adam. 2011. *Capitalism and Class in the Arab Gulf States*. London: Palgrave MacMillan.

Heikkilä, Eli. 2014. "Siirtolaisuus Sumesta Ruotsiin 1960-luvulla ja tämän päivän maastamuuton kuva—mitä olemme oppineet, mitä opittavaa vielä olisi?" Siirtolausuusinstituutti. http://www.migrationinstitute.fi/files/pdf/presentation/Elli_Heikkila_PohjolaNorden_28042014.pdf.

Hirschkind, Charles. 2006. *The Ethical Soundscape: Cassette Sermons and Islamic Counter-publics*. New York: Columbia University Press.

Ho, Karen. 2005. "Situating Global Capitalisms: A View from Wall Street Investment Banks." *Cultural Anthropology* 20 (1): 68–96.

Hoofdar, Homa. 1999. *Between Marriage and the Market: Intimate Politics and Survival in Cairo*. Cairo: American University in Cairo Press.

Hornborg, Alf. 2011. *Global Ecology and Unequal Exchange: Fetishism in a Zero-sum World*. London: Routledge.

Human Rights Watch. 2008. "'As If I Am Not Human': Abuses against Asian Domestic Workers in Saudi Arabia." July 8, 2008. http://www. hrw.org/reports/2008/07/07/if-i-am-not-human

———. 2009. "'The Island of Happiness': Exploitation of Migrant Workers on Saadiyat Island, Abu Dhabi." May 19, 2009. http://www.hrw. org/reports/2009/05/18/island-happiness-0.

———. 2012. "Building a Better World Cup: Protecting Migrant Workers in Qatar ahead of FIFA 2022." June 12, 2012. http://www.hrw.org/ reports/2012/06/12/building-better-world-cup.

Jackson, Michael. 2011. *Life within Limits: Well-Being in a World of Want*. Durham, NC: Duke University Press.

———. 2013. *The Wherewithal of Life: Ethics, Migration, and the Question of Well-being*. Berkeley: University of California Press.

Jackson, Michael, and Albert Piette. 2015. "Introduction: Anthropology and the Existential Turn." In *What Is Existential Anthropology?*, edited by Michael Jackson and Albert Piette, 1–29. New York: Berghahn.

Jahin, Salah. 2002 [1987]. *Ruba'iyat*. Cairo: Al-Ahram.

Jain, Prakash C., and Ginu Zacharia Oommen, eds. 2016. *South Asian Migration to Gulf Countries: History—Policies—Development*. New Delhi: Routledge India.

Jyrkiäinen, Senni. 2019. "Virtual and Urban Intimacies: Youth, Desires and Mediated Relationships in an Egyptian City." PhD thesis, University of Helsinki.

Kamrava, Mehran, and Zahra Babar, eds. 2012. *Migrant Labour in the Persian Gulf*. London: Hurst; New York: Columbia University Press.

Kanna, Ahmed. 2010. "Flexible Citizenship in Dubai: Neoliberal Subjectivity in the Emerging 'City-Corporation.'" *Cultural Anthropology* 25 (1): 100–29.

———, ed. 2013. *The Superlative City: Dubai and the Urban Condition in the Early Twenty-first Century*. Cambridge, MA: Harvard University Graduate School of Design.

Karlsson, Johanna. 2014. "The Truth about the Luxury of Qatar Airways." *Expressen*, February 3, 2014. https://www.expressen.se/nyheter/ the-truth-about-the-luxury-of-qatar-airways/.

Korkiasaari, Jouni. 2001. "Suomalaisten Ruotsiin suuntautuneen siirtolaisuuden yhteiskunnalliset syyt 1900-luvulla." siirtolaisuus-instituutti. http://www.migrationinstitute.fi/files/pdf/artikkelit/ suomalaisten_ruotsiin_suuntautuneen_siirtolaisuuden_ yhteiskunnalliset_syyt_1900-luvulla.pdf (accessed 14 March 2019).

Lems, Annika. 2016. "Placing Displacement: Place-making in a World of Movement." *Ethnos* 81 (2): 315–37.

Lems, Annika, and Jelena Tošić. 2019. "Stuck in Motion: 'Existential Perspectives on Movement and Stasis in an Age of Containment.'" Special issue in *Suomen Antropologi: Journal of the Finnish Anthropological Society* 44.

Lucht, Hans. 2011. *Darkness before Daybreak: African Migrants Living on the Margins in Southern Italy Today*. Berkeley: University of California Press.

Mada Masr. 2013. "CAPMAS: Average Wages Rose by 18.7% in 2013." May 28, 2013. https://madamasr.com/en/2014/05/28/news/u/capmas-average-wages-rose-by-18-7-in-2013/.

———. 2017. "Infographic: Facts and Figures from CAPMAS' 2017 Census." October 1, 2017. https://madamasr.com/en/2017/10/01/news/u/infographic-facts-and-figures-from-capmas-2017-census/.

Mahmood, Saba. 2005. *Politics of Piety: The Islamic Revival and the Feminist Subject*. Princeton, NJ: Princeton University Press.

Mäki, Netta, and Pekka Vuori. 2017. *Helsingin väestö vuodenvaihteessa 2016/2017 ja väestönmuutokset vuonna 2016*. City of Helsinki, Executive Office, Urban Research and Statistics. https://www.hel.fi/hel2/tietokeskus/julkaisut/pdf/17_06_28_Tilastoja_1_Maki_Vuori.pdf.

Makram-Ebeid, Dina. 2012. "Manufacturing Stability: Everyday Politics of Work in an Industrial Steel Town in Helwan, Egypt." PhD thesis, London School of Economics.

Marsden, Magnus. 2016. *Trading Worlds: Afghan Merchants Across Modern Frontiers*. London: Hurst.

Marx, Karl. 1961 [1859]. "Zur Kritik der politischen Ökonomie." *Karl Marx/Friedrich Engels—Werke* 13, 3–160. Berlin: Dietz.

Masquelier, Adeline. 2009. "Lessons from Rubí: Love, Poverty, and the Educational Value of Televised Dramas in Niger." In *Love in Africa*, edited by Jennifer Cole and Lynn Thomas, 204–28. Chicago: University of Chicago Press.

Maurer, Bill. 2006. "The Anthropology of Money." *Annual Review of Anthropology* 35: 15–36.

Mbodj-Pouye, Aïssatou. 2016. "Fixed Abodes: Urban Emplacement, Bureaucratic Requirements, and the Politics of Belonging among West African Migrants in Paris." *American Ethnologist* 43 (2): 295–310.

Mbodj-Pouye, Aïssatou, and Anissa Michalon. 2013. "Locating Migration: Narratives, Memories, and Places of West African Migration in Paris." In *In Search of Europe? Art and Research in Collaboration: An Experiment*, edited by Daniela, Swarowsky, Samuli Schielke, and Andrea Heister, 80–93. Heijningen: Jap Sam.

Mednicoff, David. 2012. "The Legal Regulation of Migrant Workers, Politics and Identity in Qatar and the UAE." In *Migrant Labor in the Persian Gulf*, edited by Mehran Kamrava and Zahra Babar, 187–215. London: Hurst; New York: Columbia University Press.

Menin, Laura. 2012. "Crafting Lives, Negotiating Ambivalence; Love, Friendship and Intimacy amongst Moroccan Young Women." PhD thesis, University of Milano-Bicocca.

———. 2017. "Suspended Lives: Undocumented Migrants' Everyday Worlds and the Making of 'Illegality' Between Morocco and Italy." In *EurAfrican Borders and Migration Management: Political Cultures, Contested Spaces, and Ordinary Lives*, edited by Paolo Gaibazzi, Alice Bellagamba, and Stephan Dünnwald, 263–82. London: Palgrave Macmillan.

Mittermaier, Amira. 2011. *Dreams that Matter: Egyptian Landscapes of the Imagination*. Berkeley: University of California Press.

Motaparthy, Prianka. 2014. "'It's Like Jail Here': Watching the World Cup Finals in the Labor Camps of Qatar." *Foreign Policy*, July 14, 2014. http://foreignpolicy.com/2014/07/14/its-like-jail-here/.

Nevola, Luca. 2015. "God Exists in Yemen: Part 2: The Moral Economy of Rizq." *Allegra Lab*, December 16, 2015. http://allegralaboratory.net/god-exists-in-yemen-part-2-the-moral-economy-of-rizq/.

Oommen, Ginu Zacharia. 2016. "Gulf Migration, Social Remittances and Religion: The Changing Dynamics of Kerala Christians." New Delhi: India Centre for Migration, Ministry of External Affairs. www.mea.gov.in/images/pdf/GulfMigrationSocialRemittancesandReligion.pdf.

Osella, Caroline, and Filippo Osella. 2012. "Migration, Networks and Connectedness across the Indian Ocean." In *Migrant Labour in the Persian Gulf*, edited by Mehran Kamrava and Zahra Babar, 105–36. London: Hurst; New York: Columbia University Press.

Osella, Filippo, and Caroline Osella. 2007. "'I Am Gulf': The Production of Cosmopolitanism among the Koyas of Kozhikode, Kerala." In *Struggling with History: Islam and Cosmopolitanism in the Western Indian Ocean*, edited by Edward Simpson and Kai Kresse, 323–55. London: Hurst.

Pandolfo, Stefania. 2007. "'The Burning:' Finitude and the Politico-Theological Imagination of Illegal Migration." *Anthropological Theory* 7 (3): 329–63.

Pelican, Michaela. 2014. "Urban Lifeworlds of Cameroonian Migrants in Dubai." *Urban Anthropology (UAS)* 43: 225–309.

Reeves, Madeleine. 2015. "Living from the Nerves: Deportability, Indeterminacy, and the 'Feel of Law' in Migrant Moscow." *Social Analysis* 59 (4): 119–36. https://doi.org/10.3167/sa.2015.590408.

Reuters. 2015. "Egypt Opening Suez Canal Expansion to High Hopes and Some Doubts." August 5, 2015. https://www.reuters.com/article/us-egypt-suezcanal-idUSKCN0QA24720150805.

———. 2018. "Egypt's Suez Canal Reports High $5.585 Billion Annual Revenue." June 17, 2018. https://uk.reuters.com/article/uk-egypt-economy-suezcanal/egypts-suez-canal-reports-record-high-5-585-billion-annual-revenue-idUKKBN1JD0AF.

Rock-Singer, Aaron. 2019. *Practicing Islam in Egypt: Print Media and Islamic Revival*. Cambridge: Cambridge University Press.

Sayad, Abdelmalek. 1999. *La double absence: Des illusions de l'emigré aux souffrances de l'immigré*. Paris: Éditions du Seuil.

Schafenort, Nadine. 2014. "Off and Running: Qatar Brands for FIFA World Cup." In *Under Construction: Logics of Urbanism in the Gulf Region*, edited by Steffen Wippel, Katrin Bromber, Christian Steiner, and Birgit Krawietz, 71–87. Surrey: Ashgate.

Schewe, Eric. 2012. "District Map of the Presidential Election in Lower Egypt: An Environmental History." July 7, 2012. https://ericschewe.wordpress.com/2012/07/07/district-map-of-the-presidential-election-in-lower-egypt-an-environmental-history/.

Schielke, Samuli. 2015. *Egypt in the Future Tense: Hope, Frustration and Ambivalence, Before and After 2011*. Bloomington: Indiana University Press.

———. 2016. "Can Poetry Change the World? Reading Amal Dunqul in Egypt in 2011." In *Islam and the Popular Arts*, edited by Karin van Nieuwkerk, Mark LeVine, and Martin Stokes, 122–48. Austin: University of Texas Press.

———. 2017. *Hatta yantahi al-naft: al-hijra wa-l-ahlam fi dawahi al-Khalij* (Until the End of Oil: Migration and Dreams in the Suburbs of the Gulf). Translated by Amr Khairy. Cairo: al-Sefsafa.

Schielke, Samuli, and Mukhtar Saad Shehata. 2016. "The Writing of Lives: An Ethnography of Writers and Their Milieus in Alexandria." *ZMO Working Papers* 17. http://d-nb.info/1122236654/34.

Schiffauer, Werner. 1991. *Die Migranten aus Subay: Türken in Deutschland: eine Ethnografie*. Stuttgart: Klett-Cotta.

Schwarz, Christoph H. 2017. "Familie und Zukunft." In *Zwischen Ungewiss-heit und Zuversicht: Jugend im Nahen Osten und Nordafrika*, edited by Jörg Gertel and Ralf Hexel, 141–59. Bonn: Dietz.

Sedgwick, Mark. 2017. "Eclectic Sufism in Contemporary Cairo." *Tidsskrift for Islamforskning* 11 (1): 65–82.

Shehata, Mukhtar Saad, and Samuli Schielke, dirs. 2013. *Al-'Asima al-sir-riya* (The Secret Capital). Documentary film. Egypt. https://www.youtube.com/watch?v=V_mrTifpEI8.

Simmel, Georg. [1900] 1989. *Philosophie des Geldes*. Frankfurt: Suhrkamp.

Starrett, Gregory. 2009. "Islam and the Politics of Enchantment." *Journal of the Royal Anthropological Institute* 15 (S1): S222–S240.

Steiner, Christian. 2014. "Iconic Spaces, Symbolic Capital and the Political Economy of Urban Development in the Arab Gulf." In *Under Construction: Logics of Urbanism in the Gulf Region*, edited by Steffen Wippel, Katrin Bromber, Christian Steiner, and Birgit Krawietz, 17–30. Surrey: Ashgate.

Stephan-Emmrich, Manja. 2017. "Playing Cosmopolitan: Muslim Self-fashioning, Migration, and (Be-)longing in the Tajik Dubai Business." *Central Asian Affairs* 4 (3). https://doi.org/10.1163/22142290-00403001.

Stephan-Emmrich, Manja, and Abdullah Mirzoev. 2016. "The Manufacturing of Islamic Lifestyles in Tajikistan through the Prism of Dushanbe's Bazars." *Central Asian Survey* 35 (2): 157–77.

Strauss, Claudia. 2006. "The Imaginary." *Anthropological Theory* 6: 322–44.

Strohmenger, Steffen. 1996. *Kairo: Gespräche über Liebe*. Wuppertal: Peter Hammer/Trickster.

Swarowsky, Daniela. 2014. *Messages from Paradise #2: Morocco-Netherlands*. Documentary film. The Netherlands: Stichting ZiM.

Swarowsky, Daniela, and Samuli Schielke. 2009. *Messages from Paradise #1: Egypt-Austria: About the Permanent Longing for Elsewhere*. Documentary film. The Netherlands: Stichting ZiM.

Tošić, Jelena, and Monika Palmberger. 2016. "Introduction: Memories on the Move: Experiencing Mobility, Rethinking the Past. In *Memories on the Move: Experiencing Mobility, Rethinking the Past*, edited by Monika Palmberger and Jelena Tošić, 1–17. London: Palgrave Macmillan.

Towfik, Ahmed Khaled. 2008. *Yutubia*. Cairo: Merit.

———. 2011 [2008]. *Utopia*. Translated by Chip Rossetti. Doha: Bloomsbury Qatar Foundation Publishing.

Tsourapas, Gerasimos. 2017. "The Politics of 'Exit': Emigration and Subject-making Processes in Modern Egypt." *Mashriq & Mahjar* 4 (1): 29–49.

Viveiros de Castro, Eduardo. 2003. "And: After-dinner Speech Given at Anthropology and Science, The 5th Decennial Conference of the Association of Social Anthropologists of the UK and Commonwealth." *Manchester Papers in Social Anthropology* 7.

Vora, Neha. 2013. *Impossible Citizens: Dubai's Indian Diaspora*. Durham: Duke University Press.

Weir, Peter, dir. 1998. *The Truman Show*. United States: Paramount Pictures.

Weyland, Petra. 1993. *Inside the Third World Village*. London: Routledge.

Wippel, Steffen, Katrin Bromber, Christian Steiner, and Birgit Krawietz, eds. 2014. *Under Construction: Logics of Urbanism in the Gulf Region*. Surrey: Ashgate.

INDEX

Abbas 84–86, 90
Abdelwahhab 49–51, 56, 90
Abenante, Paola 72
Abu Dhabi 64, 66–67, 75, 79
Abu Gweily, Bassem 96–98
accommodation 20–23, 44, 62; in
    Nasr 53–56; protest against
    moving 32–34
Adham 22
adulthood 8, 71, 81, 87
Ali 12–13, 44–45, 95
alienation 7, 17, 20, 47, 52, 78, 94
America, North 6–8, 29, 50, 102
Amr 1–2, 8, 10, 16, 22, 40–41, 78,
Antar 77–78
anthropologists 9–10, 55, 106,
    115n7
Appadurai, Arjun 58, 109
Arab region 5, 23, 30, 49–51, 58,
    65, 107–108
Arabic language 6–7, 22, 25–26

"bachelors" 35, 37–38
Bank of Eastasia 13–14, 24, 32, 38
Bank of Oceania 11–13, 39, 43, 77
Bhupal 43–44
borders *see* visa and border regimes
Bourdieu, Pierre 58, 110, 117n20

bourgeoisie, global 87–88
building a life 45, 49, 53, 75, 113

cafés: in Doha 49; in Nazlat
    al-Rayyis 72
Cairo 1, 64, 85, 87, 96
"cancellation" 16, 67
Castoriadis, Cornelius 109
Christianity and Christians 85,
    88–89, 91; neo-Pentecostal
    93–94
citizenship: as marker of distinc-
    tion 6, 27, 37, 105
class: and lifestyles 84; and mar-
    riage 65; and segregation 3,
    24, 37–38; reproduced by
    migration: 86–88; structuring
    mobility 6, 74, 89
Coelho, Paolo 63, 69
contracts 6, 8, 12–16, 46, 63–64,
    66–67, 78–80
cosmopolitanism 24, 87, 93, 95–96,
    106

De Certeau, Michel 31, 66
dialectic 4, 81
Doha: as a utopia and dystopia
    1–4; field research in 9–10;

moving around 19–20, 36; old
  center of 11, 35, 49
dreams: definition xiii, 107–109;
  and political economy 112–
  114; and reality 4; calculated
  in numbers 57, 85; composed
  of available materials 61;
  individual or shared 110–111;
  inevitable 51, 54–59; necessary
  to live 56; nighttime 1, 107;
  of life after death 94–95; of
  migration 8–9, 54, 89, 105; of
  normality 81; of quick fortune
  45–46; of return home 77–78;
  of revolution 33–34; "other"
  61–67; productive in unsettling ways 77–81, 84, 86, 101;
  two powers of xiv, 56–57, 75,
  88, 94, 114;
Dubai 96
Dunqul, Amal 62

ecology 110
economy: linked with morality and
  imagination xiv, 57, 59, 77, 89,
  112–114; of Egypt 64, 73–74,
  83, 105; political 71, 75, 98,
  101, 112, 119n39; see also
  neoliberalism
Egypt and Egyptians: as a migrant
  nation 5, 83–84; compared
  to a prison 69; economic
  situation in 64, 73–74, 83,
  105; relations with the Gulf
  67, 98, 104, 118n29; longing
  for 2, 77; rural regions of 9,
  84, 101–102, 105; self-image
  as cultivated and romantic
  39–41; shifting demography
  of migration from 88–89;

relations with other nationalities in Qatar 22–25, 32–33
Elliot, Alice 105, 117n23
Elsheshtawy, Yasser 3
Eman 87
English language 6, 14, 25,
  107–108
ethnicity 23–27, 33, 37, 105
escape 8, 98
Eurasian Sport Association 1, 16,
  40
Europe and Europeans 6–8, 25, 29,
  37, 44–45, 50, 53, 74, 101–104
"expats" 6, 37
exploitation 2, 6, 16, 26, 29, 31, 57,
  103, 113

family 41, 52, 55–56, 65, 77, 84–86,
  117n24; "families only" 35–38;
  of Tawfiq 5, 8–9, 48, 66–67;
  the Family Park 40
Finland 103–106
food 2, 22–23, 43, 69
Foucault, Michel 31, 83, 110
freedom xiv, 9, 45–47, 72, 98, 113
friendship 9, 20–22, 25, 50

gender 5, 36–41, 47, 65; see also
  masculinity
generations 87–88, 95–96, 104
ghurba (strangerhood) 7, 10, 86,
  89; extended 78–79; spiritual
  effect of 95–96
Girgis 13, 32–33, 44
God 5, 50, 56, 91, 94, 97–98, 107
Grand Hamad Street (Doha) 11,
  26, 35–36
Gulf, the: hyperreal urbanity
  in 3–4, 61, 113–114; labor
  regimes in 12, 15–16, 103;

lifestyles inspired by 66,
83–84, 86–87; migration to
5–7, 26, 53–54, 73, 78–79, 102,
104; social scientific study of
112; spiritual impact of 41,
91–96; stereotypes about 39,
41; suburbs of xiv–xv, 101, 106

Hage, Ghassan 51–52
al-Haj Saleh, Yassin 72
Hamza 13–14, 29, 32–33
heteronormativity 38, 50
hijra (emigration for permanent
resettlement) 6–7
Hilal 78–79, 88, 90
Hornborg, Alf 110
houses: building of 48, 54–55, 59,
66, 72–75, 80, 84, 104; empty
85–86
Hyperreality and simulation 2–4,
43, 113–114

Ibn al-'Arabi, Muhyiddin 96
imagination, definition 107–110;
and relations of production
59; and political economy xv,
113–114; as a finite excess of
the known 88; religious 94–95;
two powers of xiv, 58–62; 65;
69, 79; see also dreams
India and Indians 11, 14, 21–24,
32–33, 94, 115n4
Islam and Muslims 6, 26, 39,
88–89, 91; shifting theological
orientations 95–96; Islamic
mysticism (Sufism) 96–99,
108; Islamic revival, the 41,
92–95; Islamist movements 74,
92–93, 98, 118n32
Italy 5, 53

Jackson, Michael D. 56, 72, 117n20
Jahin, Salah 80

kafala (sponsorship) 6, 14–15, 47,
49, 116n9
Kafr al-Dawwar 87
Khaled 87
khalli walli 24, 30
King, Martin Luther xiii
Kishk, Sheikh Abdelhamid 93
Kuwait 26, 84–85, 87

labor regime 6, 12, 15–16, 41, 46,
58, 103–104, 112, 116n8
laptops 21, 48
liberalism 86, 92, 96, 110
literature 8, 21, 62–63, 73, 75
Lokraj 13–14, 24–25, 29, 32–33,
38–39
love 9, 40–41; and marriage 64–66,
75; mystical 97–98

Mahmood, Saba 110
Makram-Ebeid, Dina 52
marriage 5, 9, 37, 39, 59, 71, 75, 77,
84–85; as main aim of migration 8, 11, 41, 49–52, 54–55;
and love 64–66, 75
Marx, Karl 59, 110
masculinity 38, 41–42, 52
migrant workers: comparing
their situation to slavery 29;
countries of origin 11, 21, 26;
divided by class 37–38; divided
by racism 22–27; doing most
work 14, 26; facing alienation
but no choice 47, 52, 78

migration: Arabic terminology

of 6–7; as global condition
102–103, 106; and postponed
return 77–78; and trade 79;
as a normalization engine 83;
circular 6, 80–81, 89, 104;
difficulty to tell about 54–55;
from Finland and Egypt compared 103–105; motivated
by and productive of dreams
53–59, 83–86, 101; not new
in Egypt 102; propelled by
gender and sexuality 41–42;
rural-to-urban 86, 103, 105,
118n32; shifting demographic
structure of 88–89; social scientific study of 111; statistical
data on 5, 26, 103;
mobile phones 30, 43, 48, 77, 97,
116n12
mobility: existential 51–52; social
87–88
money 2, 14, 16, 29–30, 54–55,
73–75, 78, 112–113; and calculative imagination 45–46,
57–58; and love 65–66; as rizq
91; needed for marriage 8,
37–38, 41–42, 47–52, 84–85;
omnipresent 43–44
morality and ethics: and food 23;
and Islamic revival 93–94; and
sexuality 39; inseparable from
economy and dreams xv, 47,
52, 58–59, 61, 83, 89, 111–114
Mubarak, Hosni and Gamal 62
Muhammad, Prophet 6

Nazlat al-Rayyis 1, 5, 8, 10, 64,
66–67, 72–74, 80, 84–85,
101–102
neoliberalism 61, 63, 92–93, 109

Nepal and Nepalese 9, 11, 13–15,
21–25, 29, 32–33, 38, 43–44,
101
normality 71, 83, 90, 95, 114

offspring 50–51, 84
oil and gas 12, 71, 78–79, 113
Oommen, Ginu Zacharia 93–94

parks 35–37, 40–41
Philippines 24, 36, 101
poetry 62, 65, 80, 96
power relations 27, 31, 71, 109,
112–114
prayer (salat) 13, 22, 95–96
pressure 16, 54–55, 73–75, 105,
117n24
protest action 32–34, 116n8

al-Qaradawi, Sheikh Muhammad
93
Qatar and Qataris: as hierarchical
and segregated society 35–37;
compared with Abu Dhabi
66; Europeans in 45; migrant
population in 26, 77–78; labor
laws in 15–16; migrants' opinions about 2, 14, 34, 37–42;
43–44; political economy of 12
quotas for nationalities 24–25
Qur'an, the 21, 119n33

racism 23–27, 37
religion 23, 91–91; *see also* Christianity; Islam; God
resistance 32–34, 62–64
revolution; in Cuba 9; dream of 29,
33–34, 62; in Egypt 64, 87, 90,
97–98, 118n29; not in Qatar
27, 34; counterrevolution

73–74, 89
Rizq 53–54
rizq (divine sustenance)
Rumi, Jalal al-Din 96

Sadat, Anwar 84
safar (travel) 7–8, 10, 70, 75, 85, 89
salaries 2, 6, 9, 14–16, 37, 44–45,
    47–48, 57, 63–64, 66, 78, 80,
    118n25
Saudi Arabia 5, 15, 48, 74, 87,
    91–92, 96, 116–18, 116–15,
    117–18, 118n29
Sayad, Abdelmalek 108
Sayf 13, 32–34, 38–39, 53–54, 56
security contractor 1, 8, 11, 13–16,
    19–20, 26, 29–30, 32–33, 40,
    49, 66
security guards: ranks and salaries
    11, 19–29; recruitment 8, 26;
    workplaces and routines 1–2,
    12–14, 22, 30, 38, 40, 43, 49;
    not concerned with security
    13; not the worst off 16, 29;
    guarding other migrants 13,
    35–36, 116n8
segregation: between "families"
    and "bachelors" 35–38; ethnic
    23–24, 33; gender 41, 65
sex 13, 38; and Egyptian stereo-
    types of the Gulf 39–41
sexual harassment 36, 38–39,
    116n15
shopping malls 2–4, 19, 35–38, 40
Simmel, Georg 47
Smart Village Egypt 1
socialism 9, 97
Souq Waqif (Doha) 35–37
stability 49, 52, 58, 77–78
Steiner, Christian 113

stereotypes: ethnic 24; sexual
    39–41; political 92
structure and agency 109, 101
Sudan and Sudanese 11, 21, 23
Suez Canal 74
Sweden 89, 103–106

tactics and strategies 31, 66
Tawfiq: in Egypt 8–10, 64–67,
    69–75, 78–80, 96–99; in Qatar
    1–13, 16, 20–25, 32–49, 62–62,
    69–70, 79; in the United Arab
    Emirates 64–67, 80; family
    and marriage: 5, 8–9, 48,
    65–67, 80–81
television 2, 21, 50, 65
Towfiq, Ahmed Khaled 3
trade 79, 90

United Arab Emirates 5, 15, 38, 67,
    70, 80, 115n4, 118n29
urbanity 3, 19, 86, 103, 113,
    118n32; semi- 84

visa and border regimes 5–6, 16,
    71, 103–104
Vivieiros de Castro, Eduardo, 110

walking 1, 19, 33, 36, 40, 44, 48, 72
walls as a metaphor for limitations
    3, 69–72, 98
well-being, material and existential
    23, 83, 105
Western Union 48

Zarqaa 10, 64, 66–67, 73, 80, 88, 90
Zayd 30, 37, 77–78